# Knowing Who We Are

*Discovering Our True Spiritual Identities in Christ*

**Mark Calvin Nelson**

Sword of the Spirit Publishing

ISBN 13: 978-1-9392191-3-8

Published by Sword of the Spirit Publishing
www.swordofspirit.net

**Dedication:**

I would like to dedicate this book to my children. It's my hope that this book serves as a memoir of who God has been for me in my history. It's my prayer that you would drink from the wells of identity that the Lord has dug in me and that you would be the beneficiary of who He is through me. May He be for you all that He has been for me and much more. I bless each of your journeys into the heart of God.

Karlie – you have brought so much joy into my life. I love your confidence and your boldness. You are beautiful, smart, and special all knit together perfectly by the Lord. I know that the Lord is going to heal many through your life. I bless your multidimensional healing anointing in the Name of Jesus. I bless your leadership and your influence. I bless your favor with God and with man. I bless the many journeys you will have into many nations of the earth, and I bless the secret place in your life. I bless your creativity and innovation. There is a solution for everything! He is living inside you.

Levi – you have opened up my life to know the Lord in ways you'll never know. I love your tender heart and your inner peace. Daily, I am overwhelmed by your smile. You are so patient – full of love and goodness. I am so glad that I have the privilege to watch all the many talents the Lord has put in your life. I bless your ability to run in the Kingdom. I bless you with a spirit of wisdom and revelation in the knowledge of God. I bless your ministry unto the Lord. And I declare that whatsoever your hands will touch will prosper in Jesus Name

Drew – from the moment you came into the world you entered with strength and authority. I love the way your presence changes the atmosphere all around you. I love your strength and endurance. I love your faithfulness and perseverance. You will know God in ways that only others will dream about. Your assignments from the Lord throughout your life will be great and will affect many, and many will never know the full weight of authority you carry. I will love watching places open up for you and you walking in and releasing the Kingdom of God. I bless your destiny in Jesus Name.

Daddy loves all of you.

**Special Thanks:**

I would like to thank my wife Katie, whom I love and adore. I love who I am when I'm with you. You are so dynamic in all of the right ways for me. Your consistent strength has carried us during the times when mine was absent or not enough. I have loved giving myself to the dreams of your heart, and I love the passion we share for the Kingdom.

I would like to thank River of Life – I am so blessed to serve you. You are an oasis in the spirit. I love who we're becoming. You are all gifts to me every day. Thank you for letting me try all this identity stuff out on you for the last few years!

I would like to thank my family and friends. Relationships are the currency of heaven. The relationships that I have had with you have blessed me tremendously.

# Table of Contents

# Introduction

## Who Jesus is to you – He'll be through you

Who am I? Why am I here? Throughout the eons, mankind has asked these two important questions. The answer to these questions echo through time and can be traced all the way back to the creation story. God created man in His image and in His likeness; God breathed into His creation and man became a living being.

The first thing that Adam did was co-create with God. This is seemingly insignificant as you peruse the creation story; however, who God was to Adam was creator and who Adam became as a result is co-creator. There is a tremendous principal in there. Who God was to Adam, He gave power for Adam to be that same thing – or if you like, who God was to Adam, He was through Adam.

Jesus echoed this principal as He taught His disciples in Matthew chapter 16. Jesus asked His disciples, *"Who do people say that I am?"* The answers He got were inaccurate popular opinion. But Jesus was more interested in the disciple's perception of Him – or if you like, who He was to them. Peter answered, *"You are the Christ, the Son of the living God."* Peter's confession was that Jesus was the Son of God anointed with power. That was Peter's experience of Jesus, and Jesus said that because I am the One anointed with power for you, I'll be the One anointed with power through you.

It is intriguing to me that Peter got the right answer by saying that Jesus was the Christ. Jesus had many identities. There is a sign that hangs in the foyer of our church that has hundreds of names of Jesus. Every name is one of His uniquely powerful identities. What if Peter would have said to Jesus, *"You are the King of Kings"*? He would have been accurate, but what Jesus and the Father were wanting to give Peter was revelation. They wanted to empower Peter with an identity. Your revelation of God is a revelation of who you are in God. In other words, who you see God to be is how you will model Him. Who you've experienced God to be for you is how you will reflect Him to the world.

Every revelation of God's true identity creates transformation in us. Because we were made in God's image and in His likeness, when we see Him we become like Him. Why? Because I see Him just like He is. (1 John 3:2) Transformation occurs when I see Him. Paul says in 2 Corinthians 3 that in Jesus we are able to behold the glory of God, and he likens it to looking in a mirror. Why? Because we are being transformed from glory to glory. Notice, Paul doesn't say we are being transferred from sin to glory. In Jesus, through the working of the Holy Spirit, we are moving from one degree of glory to a greater degree of glory.

Revelation of Jesus is a beautiful thing. Everything we see in Jesus is available to us. Identity transformation occurs many times without us even knowing it. It's the normal Christian experience to be upgraded in our identity by seeing Jesus. Knowing the facts about Jesus' identity or memorizing the names of Jesus doesn't change our life. Revelation occurs or the proverbial light bulb comes on as we experience who Jesus is for us.

Information is not revelation. Revelation is new perception into the character and nature of God. Revelation is the Holy Spirit's way of inviting us to be like He is. Revelation is our ticket to receive an impartation for life transformation. It's not enough for Him to change our behavior; therefore, He doesn't call us to modify our behavior. He calls us to be participators in His divine nature. He is the fruit of the Spirit. It's what He's like towards us, and it's who we are becoming by encountering Him through revelation.

It is fascinating what Jesus told His disciples after He gave His anointing to Peter. He said, *"Don't tell anyone that I'm the Christ."* Why would Jesus say this? It seems to me that a message that important should be spread abroad. I believe that Jesus saw the danger in releasing the knowledge of fact without experience and encounter. Identity is released from God to us, and as we experience and encounter that revelation, there is an ownership that takes place in our spirit. There is a co-laboring role that takes place. There is a defining of who we are in Jesus. In our journey, we start with who God is and work toward who we are.

## Warning before the journey

The journey that this book has the potential to take you on comes with a warning. In the process of revealing our identity, our personality and our natural reality will fight the truths and realities of our Biblical identity. Nevertheless, choosing to value our personality, experiences, and natural perceptions of our life over the promises of scripture is careless at best. As understanding comes from the Holy Spirit about who we are, who we are *not* will clash with that understanding, and what we are left with it the tension of two worlds. We are so accustomed to living in this world and of this world. This is *not* who we are in Christ. When we are introduced to who we are in His world, we make choices how we will process reality. Though there is a clash of these two worlds, our choice to live in His world will begin the defining of who we are.

We do not have the right to use our past experience as an excuse for why we are not living from who we are. Bill Johnson says that *"What we know can keep us from what we need to know."* In other words, our current reality and experience of God can block who God wants to be for us. I have found in my journey with the Lord that what I think I know and have been taught for years can be an enemy of what I need to know. There are things that I've been taught that are simply not the gospel, rather they were incomplete or wrong interpretations of the gospel. I have had to do some unlearning in my life, which has been a delight for me. At first it was offensive. We all have heard the phrase, *"God will offend your mind to deal with your heart."* Yes, unlearning is a daunting task because the enemy will tell us that unlearning is straying from the truth, and that to leave what we've been taught means we have to part with understandings that took us years to discover.

These two lies are laughable to me now, but unlearning is hard. Unlearning is actually finding truth. As we discover truth, the realities of truth are worth us giving up our former understandings because as we look back, we realize that they don't actually work. It is amazing to me the loyalty we have for past doctrine that doesn't work and isn't truth. One reason we do this is that we have invested time and resources in our quest for knowledge. That is by no means wrong; however, if what we have learned needs to be unlearned for life transformation, then it will be so worth it.

What if unlearning could be fun? We get to unlearn! As more of our identity is revealed our response is to change so we can accommodate that identity. In that process we undoubtedly will have to change our thinking, behavior, and our experience of life. Why is it that we have such a tendency to think that we know it all? I love that built into revelation is the humbling reality that we don't know it all. So when we get revelation we learn something brand new and wonderful about the Lord that we never knew, because we don't know it all. Our response to revelation should be joy and excitement, but it seems that the longer we have been Christians we run the risk of developing ideas or thought patterns around something that isn't necessarily true. So we have the privilege of upgrading or laying aside perceptions that are inaccurate or substandard to the revelation we've received.

There is a very real fear in the lives of many, if not all, of us. What if we get deceived? That is a fair question, but there is also danger in living this way. I have discovered with the help of Holy Spirit that my fear of being deceived should never be greater than my excitement for new revelation into my identity in Jesus. One of the perks of having a relationship with the Holy Spirit is that He is good at His job in our lives. He loves leading us in all truth, and if we ever get off track, He will be right there to align us with the truth. The Holy Spirit takes His job in our lives very seriously. When we start to stray from who Jesus is for us, He'll get us right back on track because it's His joy and dedication to reveal and to represent who Jesus is for us and through us. We can trust the Holy Spirit to lead us. The ultimate tragedy is someone who has a theology that doesn't allow for their real, truest identity in Christ.

## Your heart can take you places your head can't go

Kris Vallotton says, *"Your heart can take you places your head can't go."* In my opinion there is a lot of truth to that statement. Thankfully our heart is capable of receiving revelation before our brain. In your physical body, truth travels due north. Truth is revealed and received into our heart. It is with the heart we believe. (Romans 10:10) Scripture doesn't say that it's with the brain we believe. 2 Corinthians 3 tells us that when we are in Jesus, the veil that covers our heart is taken away and we now have permission to contemplate the Lord's glory and be transformed into His image. These things are an activity of the heart.

We live in a culture that exalts academia. The quest for academic knowledge is instilled into all of us from early in our childhood development. I would like to say from the start that the hunger to learn is right, but the need to know everything is wrong. We walk by faith not understanding. We are not responsible to know everything, except what He reveals to us through revelation. Factual information about the scripture will not change our life. A strong intellect is not an indicator of strong faith. However, the hunger of the righteous to learn and to get revelation will not be denied, those who hunger will be filled, those who seek will find.

We glorify those who have a strong intellectual and cognitive ability. We praise logic and reason. It is ingrained in us to live rationally; so here's where it gets hairy. God isn't logical or rational! The academic study of scripture doesn't have the power to transform our life. And no matter how many Bible verses we memorize, our heart has the potential to be unchanged. God is full of wisdom, creativity, and imagination. We walk with God in trust not understanding. Proverbs 3:5-6 is a favorite passage for many. *"Trust in the Lord with all your HEART, and lean not to your own UNDERSTANDING; In all your ways acknowledge Him, and He shall direct your paths."* Trust and understanding don't go together. If we plan on following our understanding we're in big trouble. We were meant to walk with God through wisdom, revelation, and experience, not logic, reason, and understanding.

The heart is where revelation occurs. Wisdom is the result of revelation. Biblical understanding comes to our heart, not our head. (Psalms 49:3) Information shared to someone without personal revelation that occurs in the heart results in human reasoning or head knowledge, not true Biblical understanding. If we are going to choose human reasoning; then we are limited to human resource. We like being reasonable because we can reason our way out of doing anything. This is not wisdom. Many confuse wisdom and logic. In fact, some use logic and reason to excuse Biblical responsibility. This is not who we are, and that is no fun! We are learning to be led by our heart's trust through His revelation into understanding and wisdom.

We didn't get saved in our heads – it's with the heart we believe. (Romans 10:9) When we read the scripture, the one thing that stands out above all is that we can't have a cerebral relationship with God and experience Him. Most of the things God does don't make sense; that's why we can only experience Him supernaturally. We can't experience God logically. In fact, the Bible isn't even logical. The gospel isn't logical. Half of the stuff that God does doesn't make sense to our natural reasoning mind. Here's the kicker; the person, dealings, revelations, and encounters of God make perfect sense to our hearts. Revelation happens in the heart and the Holy Spirit is kind and faithful to give us understanding later.

Even the knowledge mentioned in the New Testament is an experiential knowledge. I am not an expert in the Greek, but I am an expert in the Google, which leads me to experts in the Greek. There are two different Greek words for knowledge I would like to discuss – we actually need both. The first word for knowledge is *gnosis*. This knowledge speaks of intellectual, head, and scientific knowledge. *Gnosis* knowledge speaks of lawful, principal knowledge, and we need this knowledge [1]. The second word for knowledge is *epignosis.* This knowledge is defined as the correct knowledge of divine things [2]. In other words, it is an experiential knowledge. Ephesians 1:17-20 says, *"That the God of our Lord Jesus Christ, the Father of glory, may give to you the spirit of wisdom and revelation in the knowledge (epignosis) of Him, the eyes of your understanding being enlightened; that you may know (see) what is the hope of His calling, what are the riches of the glory of His inheritance in the saints, and what is the exceeding greatness of His power toward us who believe, according to the working of His mighty power which He worked in Christ when He raised Him from the dead and seated Him at His right hand in the heavenly places."*

The verb for knowledge is *ginosko*, which is translated as an experience of coming into, perceiving, feeling, acquainting with, and it is the Jewish expression for intimacy between man and woman. This word is used 223 times in the New Testament. It is what is beyond or as a result of knowledge [3]. Ephesians 3:17-19 uses it this way, *"That Christ may dwell in your hearts through faith; that you, being rooted and grounded in love, may be able to comprehend with all the saints what is the width and length and depth and height-- to know (ginosko) the love of Christ which passes knowledge (gnosis); that you may be filled with all the fullness of God."* In other words, the experience of knowledge in our hearts through experienced intimacy is meant to surpass our head knowledge of academia. The critical point is that the experience of our identity is a heart affair and an encounter, not strictly an intellectual, scientific understanding. In other words, we are <u>led</u> by our heart, but we still need our brain.

## Let your identity disciple your personality

When our personality first meets one of our identities it will usually leave a bad first impression. When the Lord begins to introduce us to our identity, typically we'll meet that revelation negatively. Most of us live life from personality because it's all we've known. Personality is the way we perceive and behave that feels normal in our earthly experience of things. When God introduces us to a heavenly identity, that identity is completely normal in Jesus but not normal to our personality. Because of that, we resist and the negativity in our personality begins to emerge. Whether we are aware of it or not, we will choose sides in the clash of identity and personality.

Good thing that Jesus died to redeem our personality and to renew our minds. Our personality is not bad; it just needs to be a disciple to the identity we have in Jesus. When we know who we are, we'll know how we are supposed to live with ourselves and towards others.

It's encouraging how many countless heroes of faith in scripture argued with the Lord in their personalities about their identity of greatness that God assigned them. As ownership of identity occurred in their lives, transformation happened in their minds and the result was that they did things outside the constraints of their personality. Just to list a few of my heroes where this in fact happened, I immediately think of Abraham, Moses, Gideon, David, Jeremiah, and Paul.

Graham Cooke says in his book, Secret Sayings Hidden Meanings, *"When God initially shows up in our life and calls us to a specific task...He is introducing us to our identity as He defines it. We meet His calling in our personality, because at the time it's all we have. Our personality is never equal to the task. Initially we make excuses because we are underdeveloped in our truest identity."*

# Chapter 1
# Starting With the Right Perspective

As a man thinks in his heart so is he. (Proverbs 23:7) In Christ, we are being renewed in the spirit of our minds. (Ephesians 4:23) These scriptures speak of the importance of perspective. Our perspective comes from the spirit of our mind. It is vitally important that we are not conformed to this world but we are constantly being transformed by the renewing of our minds. (Romans 12:2) This book is intended to release perspective. Receiving revelation is about adjusting into proper perspective. Aligning with the Holy Spirit's perspective is a key part of coming into our identity in Christ. As a believer we can't ever trust what we see; instead, we have to believe who we are. God continuously wants us to see things the way He sees things so that we can speak in terms of how He sees it, think in terms of how He thinks, and live victoriously above everything in this world. This is what the Bible calls wisdom. All of us have the ability to see as He sees.

Have you ever asked the Lord to show you how He sees you? I have enjoyed asking Him this question for years. What He has shown me is astonishing. I think we believe that God sees us the way we see us. Nothing could be further from the truth. We have a position in Jesus. Jesus isn't just in us, we're in Him. God sees you restored to the authentic you He had imagined when He created you. We are created in Jesus' image and likeness, put into Him through salvation, and finally reborn into our new nature – don't you think we might look more like Jesus than we realize?

Jesus purchased our identity on the cross. The provision of God comes to our identity. The reason we receive blessing is because we are the blessed. Ephesians 1:3 says *"Blessed be the God and Father of our Lord Jesus Christ, who* *has* (past tense) *blessed us with every spiritual blessing in the heavenly places in Christ."* In Ephesians 2:4-6 you and I are given a geographical location:*"But God, who is rich in mercy, because of His great love with which He loved us, even when we were dead in trespasses, made us alive together with Christ (by grace you have been saved), and raised us up together, and made us sit together in the heavenly places in Christ Jesus."* So, He blesses us with every available blessing. How? In Christ. We have resources how? In Christ.

One of the things we do is constantly ask God for what we already have. Have you noticed that? I believe it's because we don't fully perceive who we are. Graham Cooke says *"We need to stop praying like a widow and start praying like a bride."* Really, what do we need? Love? The Bible already says –*"That the love of God is shed abroad in your heart."*(Romans 5:5) Peace? Jesus said when He left: *"Peace I have, peace I give unto you, don't let your heart be troubled."* (John 14:27) Joy? He said that He was going to leave His joy in us that our joy might be, what? Full. (John 15:11) Strength? You can already can do all things through Christ who already what? Strengthens you. (Philippians 4:13)

God has already laid the provision inside our identity in Jesus. I am not saying that we should not ask God for things. I love what James told us to ask for. James said – ask for wisdom and wisdom is the sense to know who we are and what provision we already have in Jesus. God's provision has come to the Christ in you. Why? Because we're in Christ. We are in a place that provision and promise comes no matter what our behavioral choices look like.

Our source is 2 Peter 1:3; *"According to His divine power." "His divine power* has (past tense) *given us all things that pertain unto life and godliness."* He's already given us all things that pertain to life and godliness. There's no missing ingredient. The blessed One is the Blesser who has blessed us with everything we need. All the resources are there. There's nothing else to get! All the blessings, all the good things that the Holy Spirit can dispense have been dispensed to us in the presence of the indwelling Christ, they're ours.

We are resourced, rich, and gifted. Our identity automatically attracts favor, blessing, prosperity, and all of who Jesus is. We have an incredible promise in 1 John 4:17 – *"as He is, so are we in this world."* 1 Corinthians 6:17 says *"He who is joined to the Lord is one spirit with Him."* The Father blessed Jesus, Jesus models the heart of the Father of blessing, and the Holy Spirit seals the blessings and guarantees them in our lives!

**If we can see our identity, we can develop it.**

The old adage says that perception is half of reality. In the Kingdom, perception is all of reality – perception has the power to change reality. The truth is that His reality is real and it is always different than our natural reality. We are learning to see the ways He sees it. If we are able to see it the way He sees it, then we can call it the way He calls it.

I love how Moses, standing in the manifested presence of almighty God, tries to show God a blind spot in His plan of using him to deliver Israel from oppression. His belief system says *"I can't talk to and try to persuade pharaoh"*, so what does Moses do? He tries to talk to and persuade God not to send him to pharaoh. When we don't know who we are, we are just as foolish as Moses in this story. Yet here is God, talking to Moses, not to how Moses sees himself, but God is speaking to the *real* Moses, the way God sees him. Then God clearly sees that Moses is not getting it and makes a profound statement to Moses in Exodus 7:1, *"See, I have made you as God to Pharaoh."* The implications of this statement can be taken in many wrong directions. God isn't saying that Moses is a god; what I believe He is saying is that Moses needs to see who God is making him into. Compared to pharaoh, who was considered a god, Moses will be used mightily and speak so compellingly that the only way Pharaoh can describe the resource, protection, and power that flows through Moses, is that he must be some kind of god. Moses had to see it before he could develop it.

Excuses make no sense to God. God usually responds in two different ways when we give Him a list of excuses about why we can't do what He says we can. Either He will ignore what you're saying, or He will say, *"Nevertheless."* God doesn't care about our excuses. What would we do if God said, *"Oh yeah, I guess I never considered what you're saying. You're right, we will do it your way."* Even though it might feel good for a moment that we've persuaded God, later we probably would wonder if we just missed an opportunity for God to show Himself strong on our behalf. God never has been defeated, He is always up to the challenge; He has considered every angle, and He sees the end from the beginning. What He is looking for when He declares our identity to us is a *"yes"* from us. He would like us to see who He says we are so that we can develop it.

## We see best in His presence

There is no better way to see ourselves the way God sees us than to seek the presence of God. There is something about the presence of God that makes us feel like we can do anything. Have you ever been in the presence of God in one moment and felt like everything was possible and that you are totally equipped to get it done, and then the next moment, when the presence of God isn't as strong, your natural reasoning mind convinces you that you can't? Our awareness of His presence has to be cultivated in our lives, because His presence activates our identity. We actually act in line with who we are in His presence quite easily. Moses knew this. When God threatened to not travel with the people through the wilderness, Moses makes this statement, *"If Your Presence does not go with us, do not bring us up from here."*(Exodus 33:15) God told Moses, I'll send an angel. Moses knew that the presence of God was the environment of true power and revelation.

We are so blessed to have His presence living in us. Isn't it wonderful to think that Jesus is in us? That's good, but it gets even better! Jesus was recorded saying that Jesus and the Father were going to make their dwelling in us. On top of that, we get the Holy Spirit! We are learning to see and be aware of His ever abiding presence with us and enabling us to be who we are in Him!

## A tale of two realities

One of my all time favorite Old Testament stories is the story of Elisha and his servant in 2 Kings 6. Elisha, living in his identity, is prophetically uncovering all the destructive plans of Syria, the enemy of Israel. So the enemy decides to attack the prophet, finds the place where he lives and surrounds it with soldiers bent on killing him. The servant of Elisha sees the soldiers and rushes to tell Elisha in hopes he has a secret exit strategy to avoid the looming battle. What he gets from Elisha is not an exit strategy, but a reality check.

Elisha assures his panicked servant that there are more with them then there are with the enemy. Then Elisha prayed that the Lord would open the eyes of his servant so that he could see, and what he saw was a mountain full of horses and chariots of fire surrounding the very army who had come to surround them. This story is rich and compelling in many ways. But what's interesting to me is that Elisha was living from a different unseen reality. In fact the reality that Elisha was living from was more real than the natural one, and that reality has power over the natural reality. The truth Elisha lived from is that there are always more with us than there are with them.

**What is reality?**

Reality is the state or quality of something being real or fact. We are living in this world, which is our natural reality, and we are living seated with Christ in heavenly places, which is our heavenly reality. We act and react to our natural world every day. We act and react to our spiritual reality every day. The Bible tells us about this spiritual reality. It instructs us that the spiritual reality supersedes our physical, natural reality. The Word instructs us in the ways of living from an unseen reality. It says things like what is seen is temporal and what is unseen is eternal. In the natural it is impossible, but with God all things are possible. The Bible paints a beautiful picture of a reality that we can't see and then invites us to live from that reality. There is a lie in our culture that, *"seeing is believing."* Seeing is seeing, not believing. Believing is the eyesight of the heart.

It is easy to identify with the servant of Elisha, because our natural reality is very real and sometimes daunting. Most of us have experienced failure in living from the unseen because it's unnatural and sometimes difficult. So what do we do when our reality is in contrast to God's reality? We should be looking to see something that can't be seen; or in other words, we should be looking to see it the way God sees it. Tragically, a lot of us create a theology that explains the natural reality. We make a nice tiny little box and then squeeze God into that box and say that God can't or won't do anything outside of this box. We have a tendency to do this because we have this need to naturally explain everything; it's a learned helplessness on our part.

Religion can't fill the hole caused by past disappointment. Many, if not all of us, have believed or felt at one time or another that we were let down by God. Disappointment is a killer in our relational connection with God. If we have disappointment in our lives, we have to immediately go to the Lord and stay before Him until He speaks to the area of disappointment. The enemy wants to drive a wedge between us and God, and that wedge is called disappointment. We don't blame our helplessness on God's development of our character. It is not our job to create doctrinal and theological explanations as to why God hasn't done something in our lives. It is interesting how many have constructed boxes of theology in response to our lack of patience and perseverance in pursuit of breakthrough. God's Word is the final say and His promises are more concrete than our reality. God doesn't like boxes of theology. He doesn't like to be squeezed into a belief system that says He can't or won't. God and can't should never be in the same sentence, because the reality is that He can. He doesn't like limitations but this world, our natural world, is filled with limitations. When Jesus came into the world, He refused to let the limitations of this world define Him. He did not allow religious leaders, the Law of Moses, the sick, the natural elements, or anything else to limit Him. We all celebrate that Jesus had a superior perspective of a reality that was superior. Why would we run from it when we are given an opportunity to follow His lead?

Our external reality is our natural world. Our internal reality is our spirit man that is in the presence of God. When we live from our internal reality, our external reality has to bow its knee, because our internal reality is superior. This is exciting because whatever issue we have in life, if our external reality is bigger than the internal identity we get to swap our external reality for a better one. This is who we are. We are learning to live from another level. We are called to live from a high place into a low place. Our internal atmosphere and our internal perspective changes our external perspective.

**What is perspective?**

Perspective is the meaningful relationship between relevant data and mental view. The Syrian army was irrelevant data, because Elisha had the correct mental view. No weapon fashioned against us can prosper. (Isaiah 54:17) Psalm 20:7 says, *"Some trust in chariots, and some in horses; But we will remember the name of the LORD our God."* I trust God has chariots of His own, and there are always more chariots in His army than there are with the enemy's.

We are either going to be overcome by our circumstances or we're going to overcome them. We will always choose sides in this battle. The circumstances are never the problem; it's our perception of them that is the problem. We have to see what can't be seen if we plan on doing what can't be done.

God wants to give us so much insight into our life about all our situations. There is a better way to look at things, and most of the time we miss it because we are too busy panicking, too busy being anxious, too busy stuck in fear and unbelief, too busy believing the worst, too busy worrying, or occupying a belief system that empowers the enemy against us. Anxiety and peace can't coexist in our lives. Likewise, trust and unbelief cannot coexist in our lives, and neither can fear and love. Walking in our identity is about wise choices. What do we want to live in, or where do we want to live from? Simple choices really, but they radically affect who we are. We choose not only what to see, but we also choose what we are going to believe and focus on. What we focus on we give power to. We will either empower the Holy Spirit to grace us with the fruit of the Spirit (love, joy, peace, patience, kindness, goodness, faithfulness, and self control), or we will empower the enemy to use his fruit in our lives (worry, unbelief, fear, anxiety, frustration, negativity, discouragement, and disappointment).

Anxiety, worry, and unbelief don't help us; they are destructive to who we are. We really need rest and peace, because rest and peace is the atmosphere where revelation is released. Philippians 4:4 says *"Rejoice in the Lord always and again I say rejoice."* Do you know what the next statement is? *"The Lord is at hand, don't be anxious for anything."* So how do you set the right atmosphere in your perception? Rejoice. You may be thinking, *"How can I rejoice when something goes wrong in my life?"* We don't rejoice because something's going bad, we rejoice because God is with us. He understands our life better than we do. We rejoice because He loves us, and we have an identity which means we have a provision.

Can you imagine seeing into the spirit and seeing thousands of angels in chariots of fire there to assist you and protect you? Can you imagine the confidence that would come if you saw that? We need to learn how to get God's perspective as to who we are, where we are, and what's happening. Our identity in Christ gives us permission to overcome. Problems lead us into a process of discovering who we are. This salvation that we have is awesome! Do you know what the best way to get favor from the Lord? Start agreeing with Him about who you are, and who He wants to be for you.

**What has God promised to you?**

There are stories in the Bible that speak to some in a strong way while at the same time don't grip others with the same intensity. There are passages of the Bible that some seem to put such a high value on and others place a high value on other portions of the Bible. Now, I'm not devaluing scripture or valuing one part over another, I'm making the point that God has given us permission within the confines of our identity to use those passages more powerfully than others.

Have you ever read a passage of scripture that leapt off the page and grabbed your heart and wouldn't let go? If you have, then you have a promise from the Lord that defines a very specific way of how He wants to relate to you. Not only that, but you have a provision and a reference point for your whole life. Have you considered that when scripture grabs you, it's God answer for your prayer and now you have the freedom to move out and release the provision of that particular scripture? There is a man from our church that does this well. There are certain stories in the Bible and scriptures that he has modified to fit him. He says that when he gets the illumination of scripture for an area of his life, he simply crosses the name of whoever the passage was for and puts his name there, and he changes words like *if* to *when*, and so on. This concept is vital in the development of our identity. We are learning to see ourselves as God sees us and applying and adopting scriptural promises gives us the reference point for our thinking, seeing, believing, and talking. We should never pay more attention to our problems than our promises.

There is a song that we used to sing in church when I was young, it was called, *"Standing on the Promises of God."* This has been a powerful tool that the Lord has used to shape my identity. So what are the scriptures over your life? What are the specific promises you have? What are some of the identities that are defined in scripture for you?

God wants to give us an exciting life. That's why we have promises in scripture; it's why we have dreams, visions, prophetic words – because God is introducing us to something more than we can think about ourselves at the current stage of our development.

I will give you a few of my scriptures. Numbers 6:24-27, Deuteronomy 28, 30:15-16,19, Joshua 1, 2 Kings 6, Ezekiel 37, Zachariah 10, many of the Psalms, and on and on. They are my identity defined by God in scripture.

Jesus had several. His favorite was Isaiah 61. As you journey through this book, begin to ask the Holy Spirit what your promise, provision, and identity passages are. Write them down – meditate on them. It is who you are and it the place of permission from Jesus.

Many ministers refer to these passages in different ways. Bill Johnson calls them *"watering holes."* Graham Cooke calls them *"inheritance words."* My pastor would call them *"promise passages."* I have referred to them as *"identity scriptures."* These scriptures are a lifeline for us!

## How you talk about yourself is so important

I speak English, and I am sure that you know that by now. I speak the tongue of my homeland – which is America. Naturally, my language matches my citizenship. I also have a heavenly language. I am not specifically talking about the gift of tongues, though it may include that. I am talking in line with our identity. I can tell usually in one short conversation what someone perceives about their own identity. Our language matches our belief system and perception about reality. The language of heaven is not negative. We live in a very cynical, negative world, but our language is not subject to this world. If I lived in Mexico for thirty years, I would probably be fluent in Spanish. Unfortunately, we use the native tongue of negativity a lot. This is not who we are. How should you talk about your life, circumstances, and identity in the kingdom? Proverbs 18:21 says, *"Death and life are in the power of the tongue, And those who love it will eat its fruit."* Jesus modeled the power of words. He would declare that *"a time is coming and now is"*, *"you've heard it said, but I say to you"*, He would heal people many times through the spoken declaration, and on one occasion He cursed a fig tree. The power of the tongue is tremendous. We all probably know the power of negative words, but what about the power of life giving words? It is a tool for life. Our language should match our identity and our heavenly citizenship.

The language of heaven is praise, rejoicing, thanksgiving, and celebration. The language of hell is moaning, whining, complaining, grumbling, and criticism. We attract what comes out of our mouth.

## Prophetic declaration

Prophetic declaration is a powerful tool that shapes and reinforces our identity. Prophetic declaration is not a magical formula hocus pocus thing. Prophetic declaration is not *"name it and claim it."* I personally don't have a problem with name it and claim it as long as what you are naming and claiming is from the heart of God and not fueled by selfishness. As it relates to identity, naming and claiming our identity is encouraged by the Holy Spirit.

Prophetic declaration is about releasing a statement of faith. Where does faith come from? Hearing. Where does the ability to hear come from? The Word of God. (Romans 10:17) Prophetic declaration is saying what He's saying. Prophetic declaration is intentional. God is intentional. We match God's intentionality with prophetic declaration. It's like we are declaring to Him, *"Yup, I heard You and I'm saying back to You what You've said to me."* He has the correct vantage point in every situation; therefore, and we need to be declaring things how He sees them. We should know by now that the Holy Spirit is very focused on the future and so our speaking about who we are becoming is naturally prophetic in nature.

The best way to release the most power through our prophetic declaration is to match our intentionality to His. Our intentionality releases the full weight of power that God wants in our life. Take your personal identity scripture list and write declarations about who you're becoming and stay them out loud. Put the full weight of your faith behind it and you'll notice an ownership of identity come to you! And have fun doing that!

## Relational Exercises

- What are your current thought processes that are working for you? What is the better way to think about that? List what you get and read it until your thinking comes in line with your list.
- Does your level of rejoicing need an upgrade?

- What are your identity scriptures? List them and ask the Lord to show you who you are going to become so you can line up with the scripture He's giving you.
- What are the prophetic words over your life? Find then and read them or listen to them again. What is on the horizon for your identity?
- Start declaring the promises and the provisions of God over your life, even if they seem far off and impossible.

# Chapter 2
# We Are Dead to Sin and Alive In Christ

I want to prepare each of you as you read this chapter. The truth contained in this chapter can be very powerful. This chapter is unlike the other chapters in this book. I guess you could say that this chapter is more doctrinally and theologically heavy. It is not my goal to scare you off, but rather to deal with an important road block that I believe is one of the main deceptions that keeps us from uncovering our truest identity in Jesus. I hope to shed light on a glorious scriptural truth that has the potential to set you free, if you'll let it. The content in this chapter has done just that for me, and I hope it will for you as well. I honor each of your journeys with the Lord, and it is not my goal to be offensive, disagreeable, or malicious. I understand if you choose to disagree with my point of view, and if you do, I hope that the rest of the book will be a real blessing to you.

## We have a new nature

What is our spiritual state? I have unfortunately been taught for years that we have two natures within us as believers: a sin nature and a new righteous nature. It's like there is a civil war inside us and some days the old nature wins out, and some days the new nature wins out. The Bible is clear that we do not have an old nature! We might have some old lifestyles and habits, but we do not have an old, sinful nature.

2 Corinthians 5:17 says, *"Therefore, if anyone is in Christ, he is a new creation; old things have passed away; behold, all things have become new."* The idea

of being a new creation is that you are a new creature – new being the operative word. 2 Peter 1:2-4 says, *"Grace and peace be multiplied to you in the knowledge of God and of Jesus our Lord, as His divine power has given to us all things that pertain to life and godliness, through the knowledge of Him who called us by glory and virtue, by which have been given to us exceedingly great and precious promises, that through these you may be partakers of the divine nature, having escaped the corruption that is in the world through lust."* We have a divine nature. I am so thankful that we are not prone to sin but we are prone to righteousness! The Message version of this passage says that we are *"Participators in the life of God."* In Jesus we are in divine communion and fellowship with, and given access to, His nature.

We don't have a sin nature because it's dead. We have to stop managing sin, and we have to start learning to live free. The church culture is so preoccupied with sin, and because of that it has assigned people a sin nature. No one in Christ has a sin nature, because he who is dead is free. (Romans 6:7) God is not dealing with the sin nature, because He has dealt with it in Jesus. Now God is dealing with our new nature – our new man. From the moment we got saved, He started dealing with our real, true, newly created self.

This is a crucial point about our salvation: for God to be dealing with sin means that He would have to have no confidence in the cross of Jesus to have dealt with sin. Jesus has dealt with our old sinful nature very well; anything we do with our old man is going to be less powerful than what He's already done. If we spend our efforts trying to correct wrong behavior in our own strength, we actually reinforce the very behavior we don't want. So much of our time and resources are spent trying to cure a sin problem that is already cured in Christ.

It is dangerous to believe the lie that we are sinners fighting sin when in fact, God gives us permission to consider ourselves dead to sin but alive to God. (Romans 6:11) The whole point of our salvation and our new creation in Christ is that we now have permission to be dead and stay dead to sin. We are learning how to live from our new identity and our new nature in Christ. When God sees us, He doesn't see what is wrong with us; He sees what we are missing from our experience in our true identity. We are not sin managers! If something is dead in Christ, shouldn't it stay dead? When we deal with it, we give life to it. Our focus should be the development of our new man. Ephesians 4:22-24 says, *"Put off, concerning your former conduct, the old man which grows corrupt according to the deceitful lusts, and be renewed in the spirit of your mind, Put on the new man which was created according to God, in true righteousness and holiness."*

We take responsibility of our new man by learning what our freedoms are. Jesus has given us a permission of freedom. Our freedoms are always more powerful than problems. How does our transformation take place? Our transformation happens as we put off the old man, because transformation comes by the renewing of our minds. (Romans 12:2) Our old man can't be renewed. It is vital how we think about our new man. It is important to remember, our new man is developed and transformed by the renewing of our minds.

If we are thinking in a negative way, we are going to speak, see, and act in a negative way. We don't deal with negativity; we approach life by thinking from the mind of Christ, because that is part of our provision in Jesus. We are free to think differently about who we are and what we are becoming. I believe the Biblical term for this process is called repentance. [4]

Our starting place is that we are right with God. Our finishing place is that we become mighty men and women in the land with the powerful mindset, the right language, and the proper perspective. We are learning to live from our identity above the problems and the sin issues of life.

## Sinner or Saint?

How about you? In Christ, are you a sinner or a saint? Sin is not who we are. Therefore we are not sinners. The truth about our true identity is that we are saints. The travesty of believing that we're sinners is that what we believe we give power to. So to say it another way, if we believe the lie that we're sinners, we'll end up sinning by faith. Having a belief system that allows for sin and thinks of it as normal in the life of a believer is anti-Biblical and anti-Christ. No where does the Bible teach that a certain measure of sin in the life of a born-again believer is to be accepted. That's heresy! That is what the Bible calls treading under foot the cross of Christ. (Hebrews 10:29)

On the cross Jesus was judged and punished for sin. The fact of the matter is this: Did Jesus pay the price for all of our sin? Did He absorb the judgment of God on humanity for sin? Was the death of Christ payment for all past and future sin? If you believe the answer to all of these questions is yes; then you are already aware that He isn't dealing with sin any longer. In fact, the curse of sin is broken. In Jesus, we are set free!

If on the other hand you believe the answer to any of the previous questions is a possible no; then you were most likely taught that you are a sinner, even after accepting Jesus as Lord of your life. If the answer is a possible no; then all of our salvations are in serious jeopardy.

## **We HAD a sin nature**

When we sin, we sin by choice, not by nature. I want to take a moment to clarify Romans 7. Romans is one of my personal favorites in the Bible. It is such a rich theological book. It pretty much covers it all – from Adam to Abraham, to the way of salvation, to life in the Spirit, to standards for living, to our role in society...you name it. What a beautiful book. As Paul wrote this book under the anointing of the Holy Spirit, he did not bother using chapters and verses. He wrote the book as a complete thought, and that's how we are supposed to read it. If you read Romans 7 alone you will miss the thought that the Holy Spirit intended. If you read Romans 4 through 8 you will catch the complete picture. Romans 4 tells us that Abraham was justified by faith and so are we – faith in Christ. Romans 5 tells us why we have faith in Christ – He is the second Adam. Beautiful imagery. Romans 6 then tells us that we are dead to our old nature and we don't intend to ever return to it. It calls this process baptism. Just like Christ died and rose again victorious over sin; so in baptism we do the same. Then Romans 7 starts out with an analogy. A woman (you and I) are married to a man (the law). We couldn't be faithful to the law which made us an adulteress. Then our husband (the law) dies. We are no longer an adulteress, because we married a man who was raised from the dead named Jesus. And verse 5-6 says, *"For when we were in the flesh, the sinful passions which were aroused by the law were at work in our members to bear fruit to death. But now we have been delivered from the law, having died to what we were held by, so that we should serve in the newness of the Spirit and not in the oldness of the letter."* In other words, we are the bride of Christ and we have a newness of Spirit. Then following this analogy, Paul says the familiar verses that many misquote and mispreach. The infamous I do what I don't want to do and what I do, I don't want to do. What is Paul saying? He is talking about what happens when we are married to the law husband. We know what we should do, but we can't; we are adulteresses. But, we are now married to Jesus! Then the next verse, Romans 8:1-4 says, *"There is therefore now no condemnation to those who are in Christ Jesus, who do not walk according to the flesh, but according to the Spirit. For the law of the Spirit of life in Christ Jesus has made me free from the law of sin and death. For what the law could not do in that it was weak through the flesh, God did by sending His own Son in the likeness of sinful flesh, on account of sin: He condemned sin in the flesh, that the righteous requirement of the law might be fulfilled in us who do not walk according to the flesh but according to the Spirit."* Amen! Paul's entire argument is that we have permission to be somebody else in Jesus Christ!

1 John 1:6 says *"that if we claim to be without sin we lie and the truth of God is not in us."* And verse 10 says, *"And if we claim to be without sin we make God out to be a liar and the truth is not in us."* The very next verse says, *"My dear children, I write this to you so that you will not sin. But if anybody does sin, we have an advocate with the Father—Jesus Christ, the Righteous One."* Later on in chapter 3:7 he says, *"Dear children, do not let anyone lead you astray. The one who does what is right is righteous, just as he is righteous. The one who does what is sinful is of the devil, because the devil has been sinning from the beginning. The reason the Son of God appeared was to destroy the devil's work. No one who is born of God will continue to sin, because God's seed remains in them; they cannot go on sinning, because they have been born of God."*

I'm not saying that we can't sin; I'm saying that sin doesn't come natural to us. It's not fun anymore, and it's not who we are. I'm not claiming that we never sin, that's why we needed a savior and an advocate. There may be times where we do sin, but the question is, does that sin make you ask the question, *"Why am I sinning?"* If it doesn't; then let me ask you, *why* are you sinning? Now I don't want to downplay grace. You've got an endless supply of it. But the grace that covers sin should lead you on a journey to discover your righteousness and freedom, not give you the power to keep sinning. (Romans 6:1)

Conviction is a beautiful thing. Conviction is the painful reality of how far short we fall of the glory of Jesus. Because of this painful reality we don't settle for a life that constantly falls short. We have a life of glory that we are destined to live. The conviction of the Holy Spirit leads us into truth, revelation, and freedom. The fact that we are *not* sinners reveals that we are destined for life of freedom in truth and revelation.

Our identity frees us from sin's power. Does your theology or belief system allow for a certain measure of sin? That is not who we are! However, I would propose to you that post cross the Holy Spirit looks at any residual sin habits as an exciting place where Jesus can be our Deliverer. Deliverer is one of His identities, and our sin habits are destined for breakthrough because the Holy Spirit inside of us is a breakthrough Spirit. God loves being Himself! He saved us, and He continues to save us. The Greek word for salvation is *sozo*. It is a three dimensional word: saved, healed, and delivered. God loves being our deliverer – He loves being the one who sets us free. He loves being the one who changes the way we think. He loves opening our eyes to new revelation.

## We have a good heart

Hebrews 3:12 says, *"Beware, brethren, lest there be in any of you an evil heart of unbelief in departing from the living God."* What the writer of Hebrews is saying here is not that we have an evil heart, but rather the effect of unbelief on our hearts is evil. In other words, unbelief is to the heart, what sickness is to the body.

Jeremiah 17:9 says, *"The heart is deceitful above all things, And desperately wicked; Who can know it?"* How can our heart be desperately wicked and be in Christ? The answer is, it can't. How you choose to view this statement is up to you. In my opinion, Jeremiah is telling God his perception, or worst case scenario. Jeremiah along with all the other Old Testament saints were not in Christ. They were in faith in God, but they weren't in Christ. They weren't born again – but we are. We have good hearts. Only a religious spirit would look for a reason to degrade and create doctrines around the idea of wickedness being spiritual.

My mom tells a family story where her mother was in a women's Bible study, and there was a specific liturgy that she refused to recite. The liturgy stated that we are poor, rotten, miserable sinners, and we are but dust. When the other ladies questioned my grandma, she said that she didn't believe any of those things. She stated, *"I am the righteousness of God in Christ; therefore, I'm not poor, rotten, miserable, or dust."* I wasn't alive at that point in her life, but I wish I had the video footage of that, because her revelation at that moment shifted a reality over our entire family, and for that I am eternally grateful.

What about you? What is your confession? What if your words and your confession had the power to shift the reality over your entire family for generations to come? I believe it does!

We really are remarkable and filled with glory, and I say that with tons of humility. The reason we can have such a high value and opinion of ourselves is because we know who we were without Jesus. The whole of who we are is all of the work and presence of Jesus in our lives. Humility is not belittling yourself. We don't have to belittle ourselves to glorify God. We have *deemphasized* ourselves to give God glory and God says, *"Christ in you the hope of glory."* (Colossians 1:27) True humility is embracing the real you and knowing you are what you are because of Jesus. Kris Vallotton says, *"The truth of God's grace humbles a man without degrading him, and exalts a man without inflating him."* There really is a difference between confidence and arrogance. Confidence is driven by what I can give out of who I am. Arrogance is driven by what I can get because I lack.

We can't afford to go around thinking we have a heart of wickedness. We can't afford to think that we are sin filled. We can't afford to be more sin conscious than grace conscious.

## A schizophrenic gospel

We can't afford to have a schizophrenic gospel (absolutely no offense to schizophrenics). We can't be a new creation with a new divine nature and yet have an old sinful nature. Either we are who the Bible says we are, or we are not. We do not co-exist with an old sinful nature. I have met so many schizophrenic Christians – by this I mean Christians who believe they have a sinful nature. That is an oxymoron. I think the leading contributor to this problem is that we think God is schizophrenic. As a matter of fact, I did for quite some time. He had to tell me one day, *"I am not bi-polar, I don't have two personalities, and I'm not schizophrenic."* He and I laughed together for the rest of the day.

We often think on one hand He's the merciful, loving Father, and on the other hand He's in a bad mood with the world and determined to punish sin. God has dealt with the severity of sin in the most severe way. He punished His beloved innocent Son for the sin of humanity. Jesus took sin so that in Him we could be reconciled to God in Christ. (2 Corinthians 5:17-19) If Jesus didn't absorb all the sin of the world – past, present, and future, our salvation is in jeopardy. Yet we know that our salvation is secure. There is a judgment day coming, but it is not in this season. We are in a season of grace, not punishment or judgment. The day will come soon enough for that, but until then we have a message! It is a message of love and grace.

There are two great tragedies in this life. The first is to reject the redemptive work of Christ. There is a real hell for those who reject the gospel message of Jesus Christ. The second tragedy is to never know, through experience and lifestyle, the great love of Christ and the grace which enables us to live in fullness and abundance. We were meant to live in such a full and abundant place of relationship with Jesus. Many stop short of living this life of love and fellowship with the Lord, because they settle for a good idea of God or a functional understanding of Him. I want it said of me that I lived this life in the fullness of the gospel of Jesus Christ. I don't want to be measured in this life, I want to be full! This is our identity and privilege in Jesus.

## God loves you, do you?

Unfortunately, in the American church there is something spiritual about not liking ourselves. Many call it death to self. I think this is a misunderstanding of what Jesus said in John 12:25, *"that he who loves his life will lose it but he who hates his life will in this world will have eternal life."* When religion gets a hold of that verse, it will use it against us. In fact, when religion gets a hold of any scripture, it will use it against us. That is the nature of the religious spirit. Remember how the religious spirit attacked Jesus? By twisting the Word of God the same way the religious spirit does it today if we allow it. It also influenced some of the Pharisees and the church culture to downplay love and promote self-righteous rules. So what does a religious spirit and a religious culture do? It will use God's love letter (The Bible) to condemn you. So the question is, how do we see the Bible? Is it working for us or against us?

So what did Jesus mean in John 12:25? He's saying you can't do things the world's way and live in the Kingdom. In the context of the passage it means that when we follow Jesus we die, it's called baptism. Our old nature dies, we become born again, and we then are with Christ in His resurrection. In the context of this verse Christ says that we are with Him and the Father.

Graham Cooke says, *"We should never do for the devil what he can't do for himself."* The devil cannot stop the Word of God. So the next best thing would be to twist it and use it against us. If he can stop us from understanding the fullness of the Bible, he'll be satisfied to keep us there, because it limits our effectiveness. He puts parameters around the Bible and calls it theology and doctrine, and limits us with it. He'll take something that Jesus said like, *"Those who love your life will lose it"* and he'll say, *"See you're supposed to not love your life."* Unfortunately many give into that lie and think that we're supposed to love death. Much of the church has bought into the lie that we're suppose to die every day. Do you know what happens when you die every day? You never live. We were only supposed to die once and that's called baptism. After that, we are suppose to be raised in the power of Christ's resurrection, and in fact the same power that raised Christ from the dead dwells in us! Romans 6:4 says, *"Therefore we were buried with Him through baptism into death, that just as*

*Christ was raised from the dead by the glory of the Father, even so we also should walk in newness of life."*

Luke 9:23 says we are to pick up our cross daily, but if you look at that verse in context, Jesus was saying that he was going to die for us and likewise we are going to die with and like Him. The second way we have to look at that verse is that the word daily is not in the original Greek language. So that verse was doctored. It was Jesus talking to the multitudes about what it takes to follow Him. He was saying that they were going to have to die. Once, not every day. It's weird that we have been taught in the American church that we have to die every day. It's like we pray, *"Lord kill me, I'm just trying to die."* It's weird, and self haters is not who we are. Jesus said love your neighbor as you love yourself.

## Identity is not self help

The idea of self-help is nauseating. This is not a behavior modification book. This is not a self-help book. Self-help is about self-guided improvement. Self-help is about independent techniques to better one's own life. Self-help is about cranial psychosis where there are usually twelve steps to a robust new you. Self-effort and determination aren't good enough. If they were; then Jesus would not have had to come.

We don't become a new creation by changing the behavior in our lives that isn't working. We become a new creation through the redemption of Christ and then we discover the new creature that we are in Christ and behave accordingly. This is our identity. We can't be what we don't think we are. It's a lot of work to behave in a way that is inconsistent with our beliefs.

We don't overcome negativity with positivity; we overcome negativity with our identity. The whole of our identity is about the relational connection between us and the Holy Spirit. He is committed to upgrading who we are into the Jesus that He knows and loves. Identity is a co-dependent relationship with the Lord. Identity is a way of life that is experienced and encountered through faith, not logic and reason.

We are in Jesus; therefore, we have permission to get over ourselves. I'm not interested in you helping yourself. I'm interested in you enlarging your spirit and discovering your identity. Truth to tell, I am more interested in killing the old self so we can see the new self emerge. We don't change our behavior to step into our identity – just like we don't stop sinning so we can be righteous. The issue is rarely the issue. The wrong or substandard behavior is as a result of a wrong belief system that is below the level of our rightful freedom. Identities are received through revelation, and revelation has built into itself the ability to change our current belief system.

We can choose dysfunction and oppression, but if we want to learn to step into our identity, we are going to have to cast off our religiosity and go for something pure and simple, but profound! We need to decide how we want to live our lives in Christ. Are we always going to live under something, or are we going to live above everything?

A rule of thumb that I live my life by is that I don't teach on problems, I teach identity. There is no point on teaching about something that we are dead to. To teach about something that we're not is just useless information that will not help us. God doesn't deal with problems, He deals with identities!

What if our problems are designed to enable us to walk with God the way He wants us to? What if our problems are designed to discover the provisions that God wants to make for us? What if current problems release to us a revelation of identity for future problems? What if problems help us discover the power we have available in Jesus? What if every problem is loaded with a promotion of identity? What if your problem has a provision of authority? What if our problems are the means to our growth? What if our problems help us to identify who God is for us? What if our problems are our training ground in who we are? What if our identity releases other people's identity? This is who we are.

## Relational Exercises

- Have you given permission for some things in your life to be alive that Jesus said are dead?
- Are you ready to start having a high opinion of yourself?
- Are you ready to let Jesus love you so that you can love you?
- Are you ready to be focused on who you are instead of constantly focused on who you are not?
- Is the teaching you are receiving focused on problems or identity?
- Read the entire book of Romans in one setting to get the point of the whole book as one complete thought. Ask the Holy Spirit to show you who you are in the book of Romans.

# Chapter 3
# We are Righteous

## Righteousness or Shame?

What is righteousness? That's the million dollar question isn't it? To many, righteousness is about behavior or following a list of rules. Righteousness is not about our behavior, it's about our belief systems about our identity. A right belief system pertaining to who we are is where right behavior flows from. Most of us, if we're honest with ourselves, are scared of the definition of righteousness because we are painfully aware of our shortcomings and inadequacies. If I was to ask each of you, tell me about the righteousness in your life, what would you say? When we define righteousness as the process of keeping all the rules, what happens when we don't? What happens when we figure out we can't, even though we know we should? Shame. For too long we have confused righteousness and shame. There is a huge element of shame that has attached itself to many because of feeling like we don't measure up – we're unrighteous. Jesus doesn't give shame. He took it from us! If we have some, He wants it back because He bought it on the cross. Jesus hates shame because it keeps us from relationship with Him.

This reality has been a very painful journey in my life. Feeling unworthy plagued me for years in my walk with the Lord. I remember a conversation I had with the Lord about feeling unworthy. He was teaching me about the subject of my righteousness in Jesus. One day the Holy Spirit spoke to me and said, *"I see that you are feeling unworthy."* Of course I did feel that way. He said to me, *"Mark, you need to hear yourself say you are worthy. The Father put a price tag of Jesus on your life – that makes you worthy."* I asked Him why I needed to say it? He said, *"Because faith comes by hearing not feeling. You don't believe you are worthy right now so you need to hear yourself say what Jesus is saying, so that you can believe what He believes. You are a believer, so say it!"* So I said, *"I am worthy."* That was a struggle for me. He would say, *"Oh I like the way you said that, say it again."* Over and over I recited that I was worthy. Then He said, *"Do you feel worthy?"* I said *"No."* Then He said something that puts a smile on my face to this day. He said, *"Do you feel unworthy in a worthy way?"* I did. And so my healing began into the heart of Jesus and into my righteousness in Him. Knowing that we are worthy is step one in the process of encountering the righteousness of Jesus in us. We know we are worthy because of the price tag the Father put on us. He paid for our righteousness with the gift and death of His Son Jesus. Then He put us into Jesus. We are so worthy of life in Christ, because He is so worthy! To say we are not worthy is to deny the value of Jesus' life, death, resurrection, position, and will for humanity.

## Your unworthiness has an appointment with perfect love

1 John 4:18 says, "*There is no fear in love. But perfect love drives out fear, because fear has to do with punishment. The one who fears is not made perfect in love."* One of the deceptions behind unworthiness is punishment for sin. The old adage says, *"If you do the crime, you're gunna do the time."* But in Jesus we did the crime and He did the time; in fact, He was executed for our crime. Our case was a capital case. In this verse we hear that perfect love, who is Jesus, takes our punishment, fear, and unworthiness, and perfects us in who He is for us. So righteousness can be defined as Jesus making us perfect in love.

If we are going to be righteous, there is this scary thing that has to happen – we have to walk in the light. 1 John 1:7 *"But if we walk in the light, as he is in the light, we have fellowship with one another, and the blood of Jesus, his Son, purifies us from all sin."* Folks that are unworthy don't walk in the light, and I used to resemble that remark. But this beautiful thing happens when we begin to be perfected in the love of Jesus – we walk with Him in the light and His blood purifies us.

## What state do you live in? Adam or Jesus?

I am so thankful that our righteousness is a state in Jesus. In other words, righteousness is a position. I am originally from Minnesota, and I now live in South Dakota. I am a citizen of South Dakota, but when I am in other states I don't have citizenship there. Before we were in Christ, sin was also a state or a position. A whopping thirty eight times in the book of Romans the word sin is used as a noun. A noun is a person, PLACE, or thing. In the case of sin, thirty eight times it is referred to as a <u>place</u> where we were before we got saved [5]. Only six times is the word sin used as a verb (an action word) in the book of Romans [6].

The word picture of our righteousness in Romans 5 is beautiful. In verse 19 Paul says, *"For as by one man's disobedience many were made sinners, so also by one Man's obedience many will be made righteous."* Paul is referring to Adam's disobedience and Christ's obedience. Christ is referred to as the second Adam. Then Paul says in Romans 6:17-18, *"But God be thanked that though you were slaves of sin* (noun), *yet you obeyed from the heart that form of doctrine to which you <u>were</u>* (past tense) *delivered. And having been set free from sin, you became slaves of righteousness* (noun)*."*

We formerly were citizens to a state or place of sin. In other words our identity was that of sinner. Then we were delivered and now we are citizens to a state called righteousness! I would like to ask a question: When we were citizens of sin (before we were born again), could the good things we do transfer us into a state of righteousness before God? The answer is a resounding no, because we know that it takes the blood of Jesus. So why do we think that now we are in a state of righteousness we can lose our citizenship by sinning?

Adam's sin captivated the whole world and we were stuck to a state of sin. When we are rescued by Jesus we are stuck in righteousness. If we are not stuck; then essentially we are saying that the power of Adam's sin is more powerful then the obedience of Jesus. Adam enslaved the world to sin and no good deed on our part could free us from sin's grip. Jesus freed us and enslaved us to righteousness. So likewise, no bad deed of the righteous could take us out of the grip of His righteousness. We can't afford to believe on one hand we are righteous and then on the other believe we are unrighteous because of sin. To do this day in and day out is dishonoring to the obedience and sacrifice of Jesus. And I say that in the kindest, gentlest way possible. We are righteous because of Jesus' obedience and sacrifice!

## The righteousness of faith

Righteousness comes to us through faith. Abraham's promises and his identity were not anchored in the obedience to the law of God (it wasn't even given yet), it was anchored in faith. Paul called it the righteousness of faith. (Romans 4:13) I think that's why the Holy Spirit had Paul write about Abraham, because he lived centuries before the law and yet he is called the father of faith. Then Paul introduces this term *"righteousness of faith"* and I believe that he is saying that in Jesus we not only have a righteous state, we have an identity, a way of life, and a place in Him that Abraham could only dream about! Abraham had a faith that made him righteous; we have a place in Jesus called the righteousness of faith!

## What about obedience?

As I have shared about the concept of the righteousness of faith, the number one question that is raised is: *"What about obedience?"* The New Testament does something wonderful with the subject of obedience. It refers to obedience as: *"the obedience of faith, obedience in faith, and the obedience that comes from faith."* First of all, the only righteousness that is acceptable to God is His own. Secondly, our obedience is not to the law or a list of rules, it's to faith. It is not keeping the rules that makes us righteous, it's our right believing that enables us to be righteous and live righteous. In Lawville, which is the state capital of sin, we have to obey for God to bless us. In Graceville, which is the capital of righteousness, God blesses us with everything in Christ and all those blessings fuel our obedience.

Obedience is acting out our identity. Disobedience is coming up with reasons why we can't be who God says we are. My father-in-law says that *"We don't do to become. We become so we can do."* I would like to add one line to that and say, *"We are so we can do."* My friend, Dan, says, *"We are in the business of doing our be."* However you want to say it, we are so we can! The two greatest words in the Bible as it relates to identity is *"In Christ."* If we sin and act outside of who we are, <u>one</u> of the most powerful things that we can do is declare that we are righteous by faith. Start thanking Jesus for His obedience and His sacrifice for us. God is righteous in making us righteous. I don't want to downplay our need to confess sin and our need for forgiveness and restoration of relationship. More importantly, I don't want to downplay the significance of His righteousness and the severity of sin. It's our faith in His righteousness that enables us to be righteous and live righteous.

The promise of our identity is not connected to our obeying the law; it's connected to the righteousness of faith. If we live under the law and dedicate ourselves to keeping all the rules then we don't need faith. (Romans 4:13) Living from a place of performance actually voids faith and cancels promise. Our identity of righteousness is not in our performance it's in His. (Romans 4:14) We are blessed to be so dependent on Christ's righteousness. We are empowered to live as He lives in us!

The best way to attract our promises and our identity is by faith through grace, in Jesus. (Romans 4:16) The gospel is so beautiful that sometimes I have to pinch myself. It's like, is this too good to be true? What if the gospel is so good, it's like a dream come true? And what if the gospel is so good that the only way to believe it's this good is through faith?

To think that Jesus took our place so that we could live from His place; He took punishment so that we would not be punished; He faced condemnation so that we would have none; He was forsaken so that we would never be forsaken, and He took our sin so that we could be righteous – that is flat out glorious, and it's who we are in Christ. Jesus became sin on the cross free from His performance so we could become righteous without ours. Wow, what a beautiful Jesus we have, and what a privilege we have to be in Christ!

It would have been enough for Jesus to rescue us from sin's grasp and give us eternal life, but He doesn't stop there. He actually chooses our life. Every day He chooses to live and be with us. He chooses to be involved in every part of our life day in and day out, and the glorious thing about this reality is that He actually loves our life and He loves His involvement in our life.

## Our righteousness looks glorious

Proverbs 28:12 says, *"When the righteous rejoice, there is great glory."* Job 29:14-23 *"I put on righteousness, and it clothed me; My justice was like a robe and a turban. I was eyes to the blind, And I was feet to the lame. I was a father to the poor, And I searched out the case that I did not know. I broke the fangs of the wicked, And plucked the victim from his teeth. "Then I said, 'I shall die in my nest, And multiply my days as the sand. My root is spread out to the waters, And the dew lies all night on my branch. My glory is fresh within me, And my bow is renewed in my hand.' "Men listened to me and waited, And kept silence for my counsel. After my words they did not speak again, And my speech settled on them as dew. They waited for me as for the rain, And they opened their mouth wide as for the spring rain."* This is who we are!

In Christ we are in the process of learning how to live in and from His righteousness. As believers we have been placed into Christ, endowed with His power, and gifted with His righteousness. Our location determines our outcome. Our starting place of His righteousness in us enables us to become as He is.

## Relational Exercises

- Close your eyes and tell Jesus how worthy He is. Don't rush this. In many different ways tell Him how worthy He really is.
- Thank Jesus for His righteousness. Thank Jesus for His obedience. Thank Jesus for His

sacrifice. Thank Jesus for letting you share in all of these.

- Now you need to hear yourself say that you are worthy. So say it over and over. Let yourself know that Jesus is smiling as you say it!
- Ask Jesus to deliver you from having to perform to be obedient and worthy of His righteousness.

# Chapter 4
# We Are Believers

We are believers. Even humanity at its core was designed by God to be believers. It is impossible for anybody in the world not to believe something. Everyone believes something. The word non-believers as it relates to people who don't know Christ is actually an oxymoron. You can't non-believe anything. There is such a thing as unbelief, but everyone will believe something. I would propose to you that the reason God designed us to be believers is because it is one of our greatest assets. We were meant to have a belief system because our belief systems carry profound power. What we choose to believe, we give power to. We are believers in Jesus Christ! We empower the gospel of Christ in our life with our belief system.

How we live life in the Kingdom culture is through faith. How we live in the natural culture is by sight. However, we exercise faith in either realm, and we get to choose which culture we exercise our belief system in. Faith is, *"A firm belief in something for which there is no proof."* Faith is not an intellectual issue – it is with the heart we believe. (Romans 10:9) Hebrews 11:1 – *"Now faith is confidence in what we hope for and assurance about what we do not see."* So how do we get faith? Where does faith come from? What does faith look like? One of the board members at our church modeled on one occasion what faith looks like. She took my hand and said this is what faith looks like. It was a profound moment in my life as I thought about the implications of what she meant. Faith is our hand in the hand of His. It is looking at Jesus and His promise and saying, *"We got this."*

I asked the Lord, how do we get faith? How do we expand our faith? He responded by saying, *"Giving hope, through love, creates faith."* Romans 5:17 says, *"Faith comes by hearing, and hearing by the word of God."* The Holy Spirit births faith in our life. It's His voice. Our faith pleases Him, because our faith is a response to His voice and His life connecting to our life. Faith is about the connection we have to this great God of ours. God thinks so highly of faith that He assigned us the identity of believers. We are believers. The message of the gospel is such good news that the only way we could believe it is true is through faith. The good news about being believers is that believing comes natural to us. It's our provision and gift from Jesus.

What we believe about God is the most important thing in our life. The second most important thing in our life is what we believe about ourselves. Our faith empowers us with the authority of heaven. My wife says, *"Heaven is moved through faith. Our faith gives action to the power of God."* Do you wanna know one of the most powerful realities that has blessed my life? He actually believes in me. Now it's a given that I believe in Him, it's how I got saved, but He believes in me. The language of faith can be boiled down to us telling God that He is absolutely right. It's our opportunity to say yes to the God who has always been faithful to us.

Mark 9:23 – " Jesus said to him, *"If you can believe, all things are possible to him who believes.""* Faith and trust were never meant to be difficult. God doesn't struggle with our impossibilities, and neither should we. If we are in Christ, and we are; then so are all of our circumstances and problems. Jesus lives in a realm of limitless possibility. And we have access to this place. The Bible encourages that we live from this place, it's called abiding. Everything in Christ is about empowerment. This means every situation that we are in, power is available to us to see something, do something, and become something. God is an interior and exterior designer. He designs possibilities to custom-fit impossible circumstances. God loves the odds around our life right now because all things are possible. Kris Vallotton said, *"I do not want to be reduced to what I can accomplish, when Jesus said with God all things are possible."*

## **We are believers, not feelers**

We are believers, not feelers. We believe that God's reality is greater than the natural reality. When we don't believe this and live in our identity as believers, we'll live life from our natural reality, from our soul, from our feelings and emotions. Our feelings, emotions, and thinking can be our greatest enemy or our best friend depending on what reality we choose to live from. When we live from our internal identity in Christ, we get to experience peace in the storm, we get joy in hardship, and love instead of fear. We have within us access all the time to the Holy Spirit which means we have 100% access to comfort, encouragement, strength, joy, peace, patience, goodness, self-control – the list goes on and on.

## **Faith is a gift**

Faith works through love. (Galatians 5:6) When you believe you are loved, you can do anything. When you know that God loves you, you can trust Him for anything. There is nothing more exciting in all of life then to have the Lord come through for us in the midst of impossibility. It makes the effort and perseverance worth it. It not only fuels your passion but it makes your whole man come alive in Jesus. One of the things we do for fun at our church is exchange stories about what we are believing God for in a current impossibility. One of the greatest ways that we can show an unbeliever the good news of Jesus is to regularly model a life of faith for the impossible. When breakthrough comes, those watching will be able to share in our breakthrough. Our life is an invitation for the world to come and experience the power that makes everything possible.

Jesus loves it when we bring our impossibilities to Him and wait for Him to speak. When the Lord speaks into our impossibilities all of our doubt falls away and we now have a promise, and we get to release declaration and lean into it with faith! Doing the impossible is who are.

**The mystery of faith**

There is an element of mystery in faith. Why do some impossibilities break through so easily, while others take time, and yet others may outlast our lifetime? I don't know, but that doesn't change my responsibility. Responsibility is my response to His ability. God hears. He is not slow, and He does not lack power. Do we honestly believe in wasted prayer? This is not who we are. There is no such thing as a wasted prayer. It's impossible to waste one second when you are contending and believing for something impossible to happen. Giving up, giving in, or settling for less is not who we are. We don't live our lives settling for less when God has promised more. Perseverance is costly, but it is one of the words that describe how faith operates.

We are people that seem to need answers. I take comfort in knowing that God doesn't violate His nature, promise, or provision to teach us something. God can teach us something while resourcing us at the same time, because most of what we are learning is that His provision equips us to get through the trial, whatever it may be. There is a wrong teaching that for a number of years has been circulating through the church that God gives and takes away. (Job 1:21) Yet we fail to understand that the Lord Himself rebuked Job for accusing Him of this nonsense, and Job's response was to repent. (Job 38-42) The Father is not a schizophrenic. The gifts of the Lord are not given and then taken back like a cruel trick.

## Faith is fun

God designed our identity to be fun, exciting, and enjoyable. Faith is fun! All life in the spirit is designed for our enjoyment. Relationship with the Holy Spirit revolves around joy and laughter. God loves forgiving us – and we are designed to love forgiving. I have loved overcoming the deception of the enemy that faith is hard, painful, and not fun. I used to believe that if it's good for me then it will be like cough medicine – yucky to swallow but good for me in the fight. I have since learned that I actually love the fun in believing and trusting God.

One of the most enjoyable areas of my life is stewardship. There is a strong connection between stewardship and faith. Growing in stewardship is one of the means of expanding our faith. Part of developing great faith is becoming a steward of what you already have. Now I'm not just talking about money – though it includes that. Stewardship is co-laboring, and it's a big part of our growth and development.

Many of us lose our sense of enjoyment in the face of difficulty. However, we are learning to love the process, not just the end result of stewardship. All development was meant to put joy in our heart and a smile on our face. The only way to embrace trial is through joy. What if trials could be fun? What if faith could be fun? What if faith was a gift from the Lord? What if the testing of our faith could be embraced with joy? What if the only reason we don't enjoy faith is that we are believing a lie about who we are? What if faith tasted sweet? What if we could live life thrilled about meeting impossible situations?

When we travel with joy in the midst of difficulty there is a heightened end result of our process. That means that joy is always a part of our trial equation. The Holy Spirit wants to add a sense of fun and joy to all of our learning.

**Living by faith?**

Many have spiritualized the term *"living by faith."* I have come to find out that living by faith mostly means this: *"I currently don't have a job, and I don't want one because I want to show God that I trust Him to meet my needs."* There is nothing spiritual about this. This mentality bothers me for a couple of reasons. The first is that I actually have a couple of jobs; does that mean that I lack faith in God to provide for me? Absolutely not! Work is my response to His promise. Work is faith. In fact the Bible says that faith can be measured by work, and that there is no faith without work. (James 2:17, 20, 26)

The second reason this mentality bothers me is that it makes people dependent on people and not God, because at the end of the day people who live in this place are very good at using their gift of hints. There are many places for all benevolence ministries, and the role of the church is to take care of people who definitely need help. But for people who are unwilling to activate their trust in a co-laboring role with the Lord is laziness. Knowing God as provider is a wonderful thing. One of the rules that my wife and I live by is that rather than being manipulated into meeting others needs, (which is God's place not ours) we partner with what identity the Holy Spirit is wanting to teach His beloved. If that identity is that God will supply, then we don't supply unless instructed to by God. We invest in identities not over spiritualized nonsense. God doesn't subsidize lazy and neither do we.

I do not want to down play living by faith and trusting God for provision. I remember for eighteen months I lived from that place as I started a youth ministry in our city. This was a relatively non-paid position; however, God provided for our family in miraculous ways. So much in fact, we learned that God will supply our needs. God was so generous with us during that season, and that season was a time of discovery into our identity and inheritance.

## Jesus authors and perfects our faith

Jesus is the author and perfector of our faith. (Hebrews 12:2) He is the rock that we stand on (Matthew 7:25) and He loves perfecting our trust and faith because He loves us. It is His joy to commit Himself and all His resources to us. He loves it when we respond to Him instead of our circumstances. He loves to be the One that speaks His strength and provision over us.

We are called the bride of Christ. There isn't much a man in love wouldn't give his woman. A man in love spends his whole life resourcing and making sure that the dreams of his woman's heart are fulfilled. We are learning the love of Jesus for us, His bride. We are given an example of what He's looking for in a bride. Proverbs 31 is a chapter notoriously describing the attributes of a Godly woman. Why don't you read it and see the identity we have as the bride of Christ in the earth. I have underlined our identities in this passage.

Proverbs 31:10-31 – *"Who can find a <u>virtuous</u> wife? For her <u>worth</u> is far above rubies. The heart of her husband* *safely trusts her; So he will have no lack of gain. She does him good and not evil All the days of her life. She seeks wool and flax, And willingly works with her hands. She is like the merchant ships, She brings her food from afar. She also rises while it is yet night, And provides food for her household, And a portion for her maidservants. She considers a field and buys it; From her profits she plants a vineyard. She girds herself with strength, And strengthens her arms. She perceives that her merchandise is good, And her lamp does not go out by night. She stretches out her hands to the distaff, And her hand holds the spindle. She extends her hand to the poor, Yes, she reaches out her hands to the needy. She is not afraid of snow for her household, For all her household is clothed with scarlet. She makes tapestry for herself; Her clothing is fine linen and purple. Her husband is known in the gates, When he sits among the elders of the land. She makes linen garments and sells them, And supplies sashes for the merchants. Strength and honor are her clothing; She shall rejoice in time to come. She opens her mouth with wisdom, And on her tongue is the law of kindness. She watches over the ways of her household, And does not eat the bread of idleness. Her children rise up and call her blessed; Her husband also, and he praises her: "Many daughters have done well, But you excel them all." Charm is deceitful and beauty is passing, But a woman who fears the LORD, she shall be praised. Give her of the fruit of her hands, And let her own works praise her in the gates."*

This is who we are as the bride of Christ!

## The rest of faith and the violence of faith

I love using my faith as a means of rest, and I love using my faith as a means of breakthrough. One of our identities is son. Sons inherit things from their father that they don't have to work to get. They get it by being born into the family. We all love receiving freely from the Lord, and we need to every day of our lives.

Another identity we have is warriors. Warriors attain through force. (Matthew 11:12) Some things we just inherit through sonship, other things we attain through battle. I love what Bill Johnson says about faith. He says that, *"Faith actualizes what it realizes."* Faith without works is dead. (James 2:17) When we put our faith to action, we will see the promises of God come to pass.

At some point in our lives we have to make the choice that we are either going to be believers in who God says we are by grabbing a hold of His promises, or we are going to sit on the sidelines and watch our inheritance slip through our hands. We are believers. What we believe is going to happen will happen; what we believe will not happen will not happen. Where we choose to exercise faith is up to us. Kris Vallotton says that, *"Fear is faith in the devil."* Our faith is so powerful that the enemy is constantly trying to use our faith against us. Graham Cooke says that *"It is better to die thinking we can win than to live knowing that we cannot."* Whenever we get into crisis or trial or hardship, what we choose to believe is more important than the trial itself.

## The fight of faith

We, like Paul described, are fighting the good fight of faith. (2 Timothy 4:7 & 6:12) A good fight is a fight that we win. Our faith enables us to fight, and when we fight we never run out of what we need in battle. There is enough faith in all of us as believers to win any fight we come up against. We need to hold onto our faith with childlike fun and excitement knowing that we can't lose. Are you enjoying the fight around your life right now? It's a good fight! It is a winnable fight!

## Today is the day of salvation

One of my favorite promises in the Bible is 2 Corinthians 6:2 – *"Behold, now is the accepted time; behold, now is the day of salvation."* This is how I live my life. My entire life is based on the quick answer from God. I also have a promise in Psalms 20:1 – *"May the LORD answer you in the day of trouble."* That's how I pray. I expect everything now. If it doesn't happen now then I have a backup plan. The backup plan is don't stop praying and believing, because when tomorrow comes it will be the day of salvation. I don't have a plan beyond this, and I don't need one, because both of these plans are who I am. Choosing to give up and developing a theology and doctrine around what's not happening in my life is not who I am.

Here's the opening verse to the Hall of Faith where so many of our heroes are honored. Hebrews 10:36 *"For you have need of endurance, so that after you have done the will of God, you may receive the promise."* Why do we need enduring faith? Because we may need to move to our back up plan. Those of you who don't need enduring faith, bless your heart; for the rest of us we are enjoying enduring, lasting faith!

Here is another promise I keep close. Romans 5:3-4 *"We also glory in tribulations, knowing that tribulation produces perseverance; and perseverance, character; and character, hope. Now hope does not disappoint, because the love of God has been poured out in our hearts by the Holy Spirit who was given to us."* Faith brings about the answer to the promise; enduring faith brings the answer to the promise plus character. Either way, our identity as believers wins.

## Appropriating our faith

When we receive a word of promise or a word of prophecy we don't just wait to see if that'll happen. Faith actualizes what it realizes. We actually play a huge role in our prophetic words and promises. They aren't guaranteed to come true in our life. We appropriate our faith to the word. Hebrews 10:23 – *"Let us hold fast the confession of our hope without wavering, for He who promised is faithful."*

2 Kings 4 tells a story of Elisha and his servant Gehazi. It's the story of the Shunammite's son. The promised child of this faithful Shunammite woman died. So Elisha sends Gehazi his servant with his staff ahead and instructs him to lay the staff on the child's face to raise the child from the dead. Gehazi does as he is instructed and nothing happens, so he reports back to Elisha. Then Elisha arrives and prays for the child who is then raised.

The question has to be asked why the child didn't raise after Gehazi did exactly what the prophet asked him to do? Gehazi had the authority of Elisha which was represented by his staff. He had the word of Elisha which represented the will and the anointing of God. But what Gehazi failed to recognize was that you have to appropriate your faith to God's authority, anointing, will, and Word to shift into the promise of God. Our personal ownership of the authority and the Word <u>is</u> faith.

## Abiding faith attracts promises

Bill Johnson says that, *"Abiding faith attracts promises."* Hebrews 6:11-12 *"And we desire that each one of you show the same diligence to the full assurance of hope until the end, that you do not become sluggish, but imitate those who through faith and patience inherit the promises."* When we live a lifestyle of faith, wherever we go we'll be hearing good words to fuel our faith. Mark 4:24-25 *"Then He said to them, "Take heed what you hear. With the same measure you use, it will be measured to you; and to you who hear, more will be given. For whoever has, to him more will be given; but whoever does not have, even what he has will be taken away from him."* Bill Johnson says, "*When you have a standard or a measure that you use and that you live your life by, this standard or measure attracts what you want. People who like good news and have decided to protect their hearts from evil reports, attract good news. Those who have more attract more."*

I love living in this place. It seems whenever I get out of town, whether it be vacation, visit family, or taking in a conference, I inevitably run into someone who is just compelled to give me a word from the Lord. At first it was very mysterious and a little creepy; now, I expect it. Someone will stop me, and I'll just say, *"Go ahead and tell me."* The reason this happens is that I have an identity of abiding faith. I am a promise magnet, and I love it. This is who I am.

**Relational Exercises**

- Tell Jesus what your current impossibility is (even though He already knows). Now ask Him to speak into that. Have a good long conversation about that. Write everything down so that you can go back later and get the promises.
- Laugh at the places of doubt in your life, and as you laugh wave good bye to all of them and lock the door behind them.
- What would it take for you to start loving the impossibilities in your life?
- What would it take for you to live life excited about what's ahead?

- What if your breakthrough is going to happen today?

# Chapter 5
# We Are Supernatural

## Jesus was supernatural and so are we

Jesus walked on water, was transfigured, healed people, raised people from the dead, cast out demons, killed fig trees, had many words of knowledge, read people's thinking, and on and on. I don't know about you, but I am aiming to be like Jesus.

If you're a born again believer, you are supernatural. The salvation process is supernatural. Your old nature died. You were buried with Christ and you were then given a brand new life in the Holy Spirit. You are now indwelt with the Holy Spirit, Jesus, and the Father. You are a new creature who exists on earth and is seated with Christ in heavenly places at the same time. We are now living from the unseen because we are spirit. Am I leaving anything out of just your salvation experience? Wow! We started supernatural and we are still supernatural. The supernatural is not something that happens to us, it who we are. We are naturally supernatural – it's in our DNA.

## We don't earn the supernatural

I have, in the course of my life, tried really hard to walk in the supernatural power of the Holy Spirit. I tried to get the verbiage of my prayers just right, and I did a lot of begging God. Sometimes we think that if we can get our formula just right then we can move the heart of the Father. God is not a formula, He's a Father. He is already moved. In fact, He moved heaven and earth for us. He is in us, and He has resourced us. God is faithful, and He answered many of my prayers. However, I am discovering my supernatural identity and I have begun to pray like a bride in love, not a widow in poverty. I would propose to you that our inability to function and flow in the supernatural is not as a result of wrong work, but it is as a result of poorly developed beliefs in regard to identity.

I love the process that I'm in right now of discovering my supernatural identity. I even enjoy the times when I miss it. I love the attempts of praying for the sick and believing for miracles. To be completely honest, I'm not batting a thousand. However, I am learning to be ok with the process of maturing into this wonderful identity. The breakthroughs I have made make the efforts of maturity so worth it!

Most of our spiritual development is not instantaneous. We grow into the supernatural reality of who we are in Jesus. If the full weight of our supernatural man hit us right now, we probably all would be completely freaked out. Living in two realms simultaneously can be overwhelming in our experience.

## Our natural brain is not wired for the supernatural

Our brain functions on tangible data. The supernatural begins in the unseen. So as we embrace our identity of supernatural, we train our brain to be a student of our spirit. Our spirit man is very supernatural in nature – it's born again. Wendy Backlund said, *"God hasn't called us to be realistic, He's called us to be supernatural."* Our logic and reason fight the supernatural, but learning to live from our spirit allows us to live from the unseen. Authentic faith requires believing in the unseen. Faith isn't blind, it sees through a lens of imagination and creativity.

Bill Johnson said, *"We can't be afraid of deception more than we are confident in the Lord to keep us from deception."* When we get in weirdville, the Holy Spirit - who is very good at His job, will bring us back. But when we fear the unknown and we fear being deceived, we become unteachable.

We are learning how to be supernatural. In the process of learning, we need to train our eyes to see miracles that are happening around us. I have been working for a man who has become a close friend of mine. He is a strong believer and I have worked for him almost six years. In those six years, I have maybe missed three or four days due to sickness. I praise the Lord for that! As we were visiting one day about that, we both realized that he hadn't been sick for six years! That's a miracle! Now we could choose to see it as a miracle or a healthy immune system. How would you see it? I choose to see it as a miracle of health and divine protection.

Miracles should be commonplace in our lives. Train your eye to see them. They are happening all around you. Your brain needs training in perception. The supernatural realm is all around us and it is more real than this natural realm.

A religious spirit will always explain away the miraculous works of God. One can always voice a reason why a miracle wasn't God, but what's the benefit in that? What that does is harden and close off our awareness of what the Holy Spirit is doing.

**It's easy to be supernatural**

Even a handkerchief saturated in the presence carries the anointing for supernatural. (Acts 19:12) How much more can we be carriers of the anointing? Handkerchiefs have a very different identity than we do. Handkerchiefs have one thing going for them – they don't have a brain getting in the way of the anointing. Don't try to earn the anointing, just soak it up in His presence. Then put your belief system around the reality that we can't be in His presence and not carry the anointing. His anointing is contagious.

## God requires the supernatural

One day Jesus was traveling with the boys and He was a little hungry; right in front of them was a fig tree. One problem though, there were no figs on the tree. The scripture gives the reason that it wasn't the season for figs. (Mark 11:13) So He cursed the fig tree. The next day all of the guys walked by the fig tree and see that the tree is dead. So they asked why Jesus did that. Here is what Jesus said, *"Have faith in God. For assuredly, I say to you, whoever says to this mountain, 'Be removed and be cast into the sea,' and does not doubt in his heart, but believes that those things he says will be done, he will have whatever he says. Therefore I say to you, whatever things you ask when you pray, believe that you receive them, and you will have them."* In other words, Jesus has the right to require us to do the supernatural. Does it bother you that Jesus requires you to do the supernatural or does it excite you? It is exciting to not only be supernatural, but to release the supernatural!

## Releasing the supernatural is not always instantaneous

There is something in our DNA that has to contend for the impossible to become possible, and we won't be satisfied until it happens. I love the story of Elijah and the drought that ended after he prayed seven times. There is something about our ability to look for a cloud of rain in the impossible. There are situations, people, and problems that have a seemingly hopeless inevitability. But those exact things are what we are called to. The places with no hope and no breakthrough are perfectly tailored for us to come in and change all that. There is something healthy about being in the midst of impossibilities. It's who we are. What amazes me about the whole story of Elijah and the ending of the drought was how little Elijah needed to know that breakthrough was coming. He only needed a cloud the size of a man's hand and he was literally off to the races. I personally think I would have needed more encouragement than that. Our perception of what God is doing is so important and it should outweigh what God is not doing. We are learning to perceive, and we love the learning!

## Relational Exercises

- List some supernatural things that would be fun. Here's some examples: walking on water, being transported, prophesying, seeing in the spirit, etc.
- Start to be aware of the supernatural in your day to day life – especially in the area of God's miraculous hand.
- Ask the Lord to help you see miracles every day so that miracles are an everyday experience.
- Pray for someone that needs a miracle.

# Chapter 6
# We Are the Beloved

*"We are accepted in the beloved."* – Ephesians 1:6

*"We are chosen of God, holy and beloved to represent His heart."* – Colossians 3:12

*"Those who partake of the benefit are believers and beloved of God."* – 1 Timothy 6:2

*"I will call them My people, who were not My people, and her beloved, who was not beloved."* –Romans 9:25

*"Always gives thanks to God, brothers beloved by the Lord because God has chosen you."* – 2 Thessalonians 2:13

1 John 4:16 says, *"And we have known and believed the love that God has for us."* There comes a point in our relational journey with the Lord where we have to pass from believing into knowledge – experiential knowledge. I no longer have to believe that Jesus Christ is my Lord and Savior – I experientially know that He is. Experiencing the Father's love for us needs to be a regular occurrence. We have to be aware of our belovedness in Christ. See, at the very least, we are passionately loved by God with an intensity that is beyond our wildest dreams. When was the last time you were so overcome by an experience of God's love that it was so strong and powerful you couldn't help but know you were the beloved of God?

## Jesus modeled belovedness

Have you ever wondered why Jesus had to be baptized if He didn't sin? I believe He was modeling a very important reality as the beloved. Jesus was beloved, and needed to be the beloved of the Father. Something very significant happened at the baptism service, which I wish happened at every baptism service. An audible voice spoke from heaven saying, *"This is my beloved son in whom I am well pleased."* The very next thing that happened was the Holy Spirit led Him into the wilderness. In the wilderness Jesus was tempted by the devil. It's interesting how Satan addresses Jesus. He said, *"If you are the Son of God…"* What word did he leave out? Beloved. God the Father cried out, this is my beloved Son from heaven, then Satan comes to Him and says, if you are the son of God. I believe that this made the Bible because when we know and have experienced that we're the beloved, no temptation can be successful. Satan will always speak deceptively against our belovedness. Satan can't successfully come against the reality of our true encounter with our belovedness in the Father. When we have the experience of the Father's love and we know that we're God's beloved, we will be able to function fully from our identity.

## Love is multidimensional

Every year the staff of our church go on a retreat to pray, plan, and develop vision for the church. On one occasion we went to a movie in 3D – it was quite an experience. The movie had many beautiful geographic locations, animals, and it was action packed! While enjoying this experience, I felt the Holy Spirit whispering in my ear that the love of God is multidimensional too. So using some Bible software, I went to the love chapter – 1 Corinthians 13, and a whole world opened up for me regarding the love of God for me.

If God is love; then 1 Corinthians 13 describes the love of God right? So I read 1 Corinthians 13 as if God was telling me, *"This is the way I love you."* I crossed referenced 1 Corinthians 13 with all the different versions on my software, and I want to read all these dimensions of His love for you.

Love is long, patient, and can suffer through anything. Love is kind, never gives up, and it is relentless. Love cares for others more than self. Love doesn't want what it doesn't have. Love doesn't strut, it doesn't have a swelled head, it doesn't force itself on others, and it isn't always *"me first."* It doesn't fly off the handle, it's not irritable, it does not get angry, and it does not do things that are not nice. Love holds no wrong feelings in the heart, it doesn't keep score of the sins, it does not remember wrongs, it does not take into account a wrong suffered, it doesn't revel when others grovel, and it takes pleasure in the flowering of truth. Love puts up with anything. Love does not remember the suffering that comes from being hurt. Loves trusts, it never loses faith, it always looks for the best, it never looks back, and it's always hopeful. Love keeps going to the end. Faith, hope, and patience never fail. Love bears, believes, hopes, and endures. Love knows no limit to its endurance, no end to its trust, no fading of its hope; love can outlast anything. Love is the one thing that still stands when all else has fallen. This is the love of God for us, His beloved! This is an invitation to an encounter.

## Practicing the love of God

John was the disciple that Jesus loved, which is interesting because the only gospel that says John is the disciple that Jesus loved is the gospel according to

John. I used to think that John was the disciple that Jesus loved the most. But then I found that it was just in the gospel of John where it recorded that. I always found that funny, but I never knew that there was something very profound about John calling himself the disciple that Jesus loved.

One day the Holy Spirit had the phrase, *"The disciple whom Jesus loved"* going around in my head, and that usually happens when the Lord wants to speak something to me. So I asked why John wrote that he was the disciple that Jesus loved. The Holy Spirit said this, *"Jesus loved all the twelve disciples, but John knew it."* In other words, John practiced the love of Jesus for him.

I have used this illustration in our church. We have four pastors, myself included. When it is my turn to preach, I will say something like this, *"Pastor Clay, Pastor Dan, Pastor Jeff, and the pastor whom Jesus loved had a good meeting today."* Jesus loves all of us the same, but I am practicing the love of Jesus for myself. I have found in my life that good things happen to people who know and experience the love of Jesus for themselves. This may seem silly, but we need to regularly be practicing the love of God for us in a variety of ways every day. God wants our identity on unshakeable ground. He wants our identity grounded on the confidence of the love of God for us.

**Love is invincible and unfailing**

Lack of faith isn't just a belief issue, it's a love issue. Poor perception is a faith issue, but lack of faith is a love issue, because faith works through love. (Galatians 5:6) We don't just perceive the love of God, we encounter it. What if being more than a conqueror means that we are falling more in love with Jesus and our love scares the devil away?

Love never fails. (1 Corinthians 13:8) What if inside the provision of His unfailing love was everything we need for every obstacle or problem for the rest of our lives? What if another part of that provision enabled us to be unfailing? I love asking these questions. Jesus paid a high price for us to freely receive these blessings. We need to ensure that He gets the most from His sacrifice, and that we get the most from what He already paid for. Jesus paid a price for us to be untouchable, unreachable, and invincible. We were created for love, conceived in love, and made for love.

Song of Songs 8:6-7 (The Message) says, *"Love is invincible facing danger and death. Passion laughs at the terrors of hell. The fire of love stops at nothing— it sweeps everything before it. Flood waters can't drown love, torrents of rain can't put it out. Love can't be bought, love can't be sold— it's not to be found in the marketplace."*

1 John 5:18-19 (The Message) says, *"We know that none of the God-begotten makes a practice of sin. The God-begotten are also the God-protected. The Evil One can't lay a hand on them. We know that we are held firm by God; it's only the people of the world who continue in the grip of the Evil One."* (emphasis mine)

Isaiah 49:15-17 says, *"Can a woman forget her nursing child, And not have compassion on the son of her womb? Surely they may forget, Yet I will not forget you. See, I have inscribed you on the palms of My hands; Your walls are continually before Me. Your sons shall make haste; Your destroyers and those who laid you waste Shall go away from you."*

## You are His delight

God's delight is in the sons of men. (Proverbs 8:31) Have you ever had the Holy Spirit tell you that He is absolutely delighted in you? If you haven't, I recommend that you try to ask Him and see what He says!

Our relationship with God was meant to be delightful. The delight starts in Him, gets revealed to us, and then becomes who we are. I other words, you could say that we recognize God's delight in us; then we become delighted, and then delightful.

What happens when we don't live from a place of God's delight? We will live from a place of purposeful function and duty. That's not who we are. Duty is not a very good substitution for delight. It is not our duty to go to heaven, and when we get there I don't think the Father is going to give us a duty. In the presence of delight there is no duty. God wants us to be with Him in such a way that puts a smile on our face, and everything that we do for Him is delightful.

## Grieving the Holy Spirit

The way we grieve the heart of the Holy Spirit is that we fail to not become who He has made provision for us to become. I think we often believe God is mad at us because of the wrong choices we've made or the wrong habits we have. But, the Lord's dealt with that in Jesus, and the only grief He has is when we fail to see and experience who we are in Jesus. We have an abundant life of fullness available right now and when we don't understand that, He's grieved. So we're coming into an experiential knowledge of that. The very bedrock of who we are in Jesus is we are the beloved. We are meant to live our Christian lives with passion and zeal – excited about discovering who we are. God is our friend, how cool is that? Only a religious spirit would try to keep us deceived and distant from the nature of God.

So how do we hear His voice? We have a list of what He sounds like. I use this list all the time; it's very handy! Galatians 5:22-23 – *"But the fruit of the Spirit is love, joy, peace, longsuffering, kindness, goodness, faithfulness, gentleness, self-control."* This is who God is for us, and this is what He sounds like – anything else would not be God. His voice matches His nature!

**The power of love**

We are loved perfectly. Many have been brought up to believe that we need to give to the Lord, but I've found that the great givers are the ones who have learned how to receive. The more we receive form the Lord, the more we can give. Peter put it this way, *"Such as I have, I give you."*

Romans 8:38-39 says, *"For I am persuaded that neither death nor life, nor angels nor principalities nor powers, nor things present nor things to come, nor height nor depth, nor any other created thing, shall be able to separate us from the love of God which is in Christ Jesus our Lord."*

There is no separating the beloved from the love of God in Christ. There are a number of things that will try however. This passage is key to being fully persuaded in our belovedness. Paul makes a remarkable statement that death and life can't detach us from the love of God. Nothing living or nothing dead can get between the love of God for us. The demonic ruler and no created being can break up this love of God. Nothing now or in the future can divide us from this perfect love. Today we can't be disconnected from His love, tomorrow we can't be disconnected from His love, and at no future point can we be separated from His love. Nothing above us or below us, nothing high or low, nothing thinkable and nothing unthinkable can separate us from this astonishing love. The love of God is intentional, direct, remarkable, immeasurable, unstoppable, unbreakable, irretractable, and unbeatable. I am attempting to put vocabulary to the wonder of His loving nature and His love for us, but even the power of words come short in describing a love that is indescribable. This reality is our experience and our life in Christ.

## Relational Exercises

- Have you ever heard the Father say to you, *"You are my beloved and I am so pleased with you."*?
- If not, right now close your eyes and ask Him to do that, He's so excited! Then ask Him what else do you want to tell me?
- Ask Him to tell you something else that He loves about you. Make a list!

# Chapter 7
# We Are Receivers

The means to our identity and our life in Christ Jesus is our ability to receive from Him. The principal of receiving from the Lord is fourfold. First, everything that you need God has. Secondly, God has it all. Thirdly, we have access to it. Finally, everything that God wants from us, He'll give to us.

God is love. Where does love come from? God right? So how can we love? We receive it from God because He's the only one who has it. So how much of God's love do we have access to? We have access to as much love from the Father as we want. Scripture says that His love has been shed abroad in our hearts. (Romans 5:5) Now, as Christians God commands us to love the Lord with all our heart, soul, mind, and strength. How do we do that if we don't have any love? We love God because He first loved us. (1 John 4:19) He loved us with all of His heart, soul, mind, and strength. He loves us the same way He requires it from us.

I have come to the revelation that every command is a promised place of provision from the Father. If God commands something of us; then He'll resource us to do that very thing. In the case of the greatest commandment: to love God with our heart, soul, mind, and strength – the four places we are to love God from is a mirror of His love for us. He gives us love from His heart, soul, mind, and strength, so we can love Him with the love He has given us. In other words, as we come to experience this great love, we love Him with the provision of love that He has given to us. What a great love we have in our Father God!

Life in Christ is about receiving from Him. Everything we need we receive. Many have gone wrong trying to work for God in order to give Him something that He would want. That's silly because God doesn't need anything. He has it all. This is why performance based relationship with God doesn't work. We don't perform our way into acceptance and love with God; we already have it in Jesus. If we don't, it's because we didn't receive it from Him.

All the promises of God are invitations to an encounter with Him when He gives us something, and then we give it to others and back to Him. The promises of God have encounters built into them. It is hard and tiring to run with the promises of God without encountering Him (so that we can receive it). Let me give you an example: How do you get money from your bank account? You make a withdrawal. It is essentially the same process when we receive from the Lord. When we need something, we encounter Him, we take a promissory note to the Holy Spirit, we take Him our promise, and then there is a payment to us. Receiving from God is so very important in our lives in Christ. It is possible that some of us run around in life bankrupt, because we haven't perfected the art of receiving from the Lord. It is also possible that one of the reasons we don't receive from Him is because we feel like we don't deserve to receive from Him. We are only able to receive what we think we're worthy of. The value the Father has put on our lives was the price of His Son Jesus

**<u>All three members of the trinity are working to make sure we get our provision!</u>**

God loves being your provider. I like to think of it this way. The Father loves making provision in Jesus, who secured the provision, and the Holy Spirit is the one who reveals the provision and gives the provision. What a team! Think about what the Father and Jesus are doing while the Holy Spirit is giving you a provision. I would like to think that they are smiling ear to ear.

The heart of God is full of things for us. He really is a God of abundance and fullness, and the only way to live in and with Him is in full abundance. One of the reasons Jesus came to earth was so that we could have life abundantly. (John 10:10)

God is a jealous God. When it comes to our identity as receivers, He is jealous. We all know that no one can meet our needs like God, but have you thought that God doesn't want anyone meeting our needs but Him? Please don't hear that last statement wrong. I love being generous with people and I love meeting needs, it's my identity. However, there is no substitute for God's ability to meet our own needs personally. He wants to be our source, and He is jealous about that. That's why we have so many promises.

All of the promises of Jesus are yes and amen. (2 Corinthians 1:20) He provides the yes and we are responsible for the amen. Amen is a term that means, *"so be it."* We are learning how to receive the *"yes"* of Jesus. When's the last time you've heard Jesus say, *"Yes?"* I love how 2 Corinthians 1:20 continues and says that the "*yes*" of promise released to our "*amen*" is glorious, and that the Father establishes it and the Holy Spirit seals it in our hearts as a guarantee. (2 Corinthians 1:21-22)

## God's identity is giver

One of the names of God is Jehovah Jireh, which means, *"The Lord will provide."* *"Jireh"* translates into *"provide"* which is a word with wonderful Latin roots. *"Pro"* means *"before"* and *"video"* means *"to see".* So the full meaning of *"provider"* means to see in advance or before the need is known. God is preparing provision before we know that there is even a need. (Genesis 22:1-14)

As a father, I love resourcing and providing for my kids. My wife and I have several financial plans that we are acting on for their inheritance. We know that there are many future financial needs in their lives, and because of our love for them and our intentionality, we are laying up provision for their futures. It's one thing to provide for immediate need; it's another thing to have provision waiting before there is even a need. God is perfect in His provision for our lives.

Hebrews 7:7 says the *"the less is blessed by the greater."* In other words, our blessing comes from the greatness of God. When Jesus went to wash His disciples feet, what was Peter's response? *"No Lord, I should wash Your feet."* Then Jesus says, *"If I don't wash your feet you do not have anything to do with me."* Then Peter says, *"Wash my whole body then."* (John 13) Our Lord loves to give. The more you receive from Him, the more it delights Him.

I love the story of the woman at the well. Jesus sent His disciples to town for food because He was hungry. Jesus sat at the well because He was tired. Then, the woman came to the well with a bucket. He then ministered living water to her, and she left full even though Jesus was the one in need. Shouldn't she have been the one to minister to Jesus in His need? When the disciples came back with food, what did Jesus say?

*"I have food to eat that you do not even know of."* (John 4:32) He was refreshed like He had already eaten. What happened? The moment the woman came and took from Him, even though He was tired, Jesus was instantly refreshed! We actually refresh the Lord when we take from Him! The more we take from the Lord, the more delighted He is.

## Salvation was just the beginning of receiving

We received the gift of salvation from Jesus Christ. The Bible puts it this way – we believe, we confess, and we receive. How we attained salvation is how we sustain our salvation. We are believers, confessing our promises, and receiving our breakthroughs! Our belief, confession, and our ability to receive is literally a matter of life and breath! I like what Mary said when she received the promise to be the mother of Jesus. Luke 1:38 – *"Let it be to me according to your word."* God is intentional – intentional people take the initiative. I am married to a highly intentional woman who makes a lifestyle out of taking the initiative. She is a certified public accountant – that's what they do because it's who they are. She has taught me what intentionality looks like at a higher level.

When God comes to us, He comes with a word and when He gives that word, He is waiting for ownership – or if you like, an amen. One of the best ways to provide an amen is through declaration. Declaration is us telling God that we believe what He promised us. Our declaration is our confession. Confessing that Jesus is Lord and that God raised Him from the dead was connected to our receiving salvation. Our confession, or in other words our declaration, is also connected to our receiving His provision.

## What we receive from the Lord returns to Him

I want you to read this lengthy portion of scripture and look at it as a description of our receiving from the Lord.

*Isaiah 55:1-13 "Ho! Everyone who thirsts, Come to the waters; And you who have no money, Come, buy and eat. Yes, come, buy wine and milk Without money and without price.*
*Why do you spend money for what is not bread, And your wages for what does not satisfy? Listen carefully to Me, and eat what is good, And let your soul delight itself in abundance.*
*Incline your ear, and come to Me. Hear, and your soul shall live; And I will make an everlasting covenant with you-- The sure mercies of David.*
*Indeed I have given him as a witness to the people, A leader and commander for the people.*
*Surely you shall call a nation you do not know, And nations who do not know you shall run to you, Because of the LORD your God, And the Holy One of Israel; For He has glorified you."*
*Seek the LORD while He may be found, Call upon Him while He is near.*
*Let the wicked forsake his way, And the unrighteous man his thoughts; Let him return to the LORD, And He will have mercy on him; And to our God, For He will abundantly pardon.*
*"For My thoughts are not your thoughts, Nor are your ways My ways," says the LORD.*
*"For as the heavens are higher than the earth, So are My ways higher than your ways, And My thoughts than your thoughts.*
*"For as the rain comes down, and the snow from heaven, And do not return there, But water the earth, And make it bring forth and bud, That it may give seed to the sower And bread to the eater,*
*So shall My word be that goes forth from My mouth; It shall not return to Me void, But it shall accomplish what*

*I please, And it shall prosper in the thing for which I sent it.*
*"For you shall go out with joy, And be led out with peace; The mountains and the hills Shall break forth into singing before you, And all the trees of the field shall clap their hands.*
*Instead of the thorn shall come up the cypress tree, And instead of the brier shall come up the myrtle tree; And it shall be to the LORD for a name, For an everlasting sign that shall not be cut off."*

I would like to point out a few truths from this passage. Isaiah is describing a cycle of provision. Rain comes down, waters the earth, produces fruit, gives seed, makes bread, and all this returns to the Lord, but it doesn't return void. Our provision is like the water cycle. The Word of God comes to us from God, does something on the inside of us, and then it goes back to God through our life. The earth gives back to heaven what heaven gives it, and in the same way, we are to give back to God what He has given us.

Whatever God wants from us, He will give it to us. I would think that we all as Christians would agree that the commands of the Lord are of utmost necessity – we need to keep them. Well God has a promised provision for that as well, *"And my God shall supply all your need according to His riches in glory by Christ Jesus."* (Philippians 4:13) God doesn't require anything from us that He isn't first prepared to give to us. What if a command from God is a promise and a provision at the same time? We receive what God requires of us!

James 1:17 says, *"Every good gift and every perfect gift is from above, and comes down from the Father of lights, with whom there is no variation or shadow of turning."* Romans 11:35 says, *"Or who has first given to Him And it shall be repaid to him?" For <u>from</u> Him and <u>through</u> Him and <u>to</u> Him are all things."* God pours into our life, makes something right in our life, and then we give back to God what He gave us.

What is your need right now? It's important to define need. One thing I can guarantee you is that God has a promised provision for that need. Our instinct to need is to pray first. There is no doubt that our asking is vital! However, thanksgiving plays a significant role in our receiving. (1 Timothy 4:4) Faith plays a significant role in our receiving as well. (Matthew 21:22) Along with our asking we need to get into thanksgiving, faith, and perseverance.

**Receiving from the Names of Jesus**

One of the ladies in our church gave me a wonderful gift. She gave me three different articles of the names of Jesus and who we are in Christ. The first is *"Names, Titles, and Descriptions of God."* The second is the *"Alphabet of who you are in Christ."* The third is called, *"Who I am."* I use these often. Whenever I have a problem or a need, I like going through the list with the Holy Spirit and asking Him who Jesus is going to be for me in the midst of the problem. Once I find it, I have a reference point of who Jesus is for me right now and I can start developing that identity. Then, every day I can go to Jesus and say, *"Amen"* to His identity and take a position of receiving instead of struggle.

What if we had the ability to live in a place of fullness and abundance? What if we had the ability to start our life and solve our problems in life with fullness and abundance? What if Jesus is waiting right now for our amen to be added to His yes so that the Father can establish it and the Holy Spirit can seal it and guarantee it?

## Relational Exercises

- Find a list of the names, titles, and descriptions of God. Match His identity to your problem.
- Start to list out the descriptions of your identity in Jesus.
- Read the *"I am"* statements of Jesus.
- What are your *"I am"* statements? Make a list of your *"I am"* statements.
- What is at least one thing that God has spoken into your current situations that you have to say *"Amen"* to? Ok, go ahead and say it!

# Chapter 8
# We Are Healed

## The pioneers and stewards of God's grace!

I want to honor some of the pioneers who have had to work so hard to restore the nature of Jesus to His church. Many men and women of God have stewarded wonderfully the grace of Jesus in regard to healing. I hope that my life and ministry to this world in representing Jesus is honoring to the resistance and isolation they endured to preserve such wonderful truths. I think of Smith Wigglesworth, Aimee Semple McPherson, Kathryn Kuhlman, John G. Lake, Oral Roberts, Kenneth Hagin, Charles Capps, Benny Hinn, Randy Clark, and Bill Johnson to name a few. The grief that these wonderful saints of the Lord must have had, or still experience, around a truth and a reality so wonderful yet so misunderstood, is heart wrenching for me to think about. I honor those who are still alive, and those who are now in the grandstands of heaven looking down. Thank you.

## Where is our trust? In the nature and name of Jesus or our lack of experience?

I briefly discussed earlier that the Greek word for salvation was *sozo*. *Sozo* is a three dimensional word that means: saved, healed, and delivered. Forgiveness and healing run together in the same stream throughout scripture; where healing is mentioned, so is forgiveness. Most of us have faith for forgiveness, and see that forgiveness is an attainable, scriptural promise. When we ask for forgiveness we ask in faith, believing that we are about to receive forgiveness because of the wonderful grace of God to forgive sin. For some reason though, when it comes to healing, we have a difficult time believing that it is just as attainable and promised as forgiveness. When we ask for healing, we are also to ask in faith and believe that we receive it.

Jesus is also Jehovah Rophe – which means *"our healer."* If our healer is one of His names, then it's also His nature. It's His nature to heal! I choose to celebrate this identity of Jesus. We all know that there is so much controversy around the subject of healing. In my opinion the main controversy, and frankly what keeps many from receiving their healing, is that they tried and they didn't get instantly healed. So in turn they carelessly decided to write their own theology to define who Jesus is based on their own experience.

I personally can't think of anything more reckless and irresponsible – I say that with all due respect and kindness. It's hard to wrap my mind and heart around the arrogance of some to take what they've not experienced and superimpose their failed attempt over embracing the nature and name of Jesus. Beloved, it has cost us our inheritance! We owe it to Jesus and the world to represent who Jesus is in our identity.

Biblically you cannot separate salvation and healing. They are two peas in the same pod. There is much we don't understand about why healing manifests easier for some, and seemingly not at all for others. It isn't my responsibility to reinterpret the pages of scripture to accommodate my experience – that is what is commonly referred to as heresy. Graham Cooke has a definition of heresy that I like. He said, *"You can recognize heresy because it's something that only benefits the devil."* It is bewildering to me how many have blamed God for sickness and disease. In the pursuit of understanding, some have carelessly blamed the one person (Jesus) who should never be blamed for sickness and disease. In fact, God is the opposite. He is the One who heals our diseases.

## God hates sickness

We all know that God hates sin, but God also hates sickness. Knowing that God hates sickness is one of the greatest ways to be free of sickness. God put the sin of humanity, the curse of humanity, and the sickness of humanity on Jesus at the cross; therefore, we know that God hates sickness. God hated everything that came on Jesus when He hung on the cross. We must be contending against the right for sin, the curse, and sickness to exist in our life!

## Jesus loves healing

We live in a world where sickness and disease are rampant. Yet how much of the sickness in this world is at the hand of man? There is pollution, preservatives, pesticides, toxic waste, radiation, and the list goes on and on. Isn't it interesting that the moment someone gets sick, no one blames any of these factors? I find it equally interesting that when someone needs healing, calling for supernatural healing is the last thing on the list. It's like, all we can do is pray. I know that it grieves the Lord too when we take signs, wonders, and healing and relegate them to a former time and nullify our need for them because we have the Bible now. I personally think much of the church lives in a condition of learned helplessness. Assigning healing to God's sovereign decision when He has already decided on the issue of healing in the personal of Jesus would be careless. Would we honestly believe that God would decide not to forgive someone when the cried out to Him in their need?

Identity is a big deal to Jesus. He is the Lord and He doesn't change who He is. Hebrews 13:8 says, *"Jesus*

*Christ is the same yesterday, today, and forever."* This means He healed yesterday, He heals today, and He will heal forever. He is the same as He was two thousand years ago when He traveled the earth healing the multitudes. *"Jesus went about all the cities and villages, teaching in their synagogues, preaching the gospel of the kingdom, and healing every sickness and every disease."* (Matthew 9:35)

**What does the Bible say?**

He is healer – He loves to heal. On top of that, scripture speaks of healing all throughout Bible. *"The whole multitude sought to touch Him, for power went out from Him and healed them all."* (Luke 6:19) My personal favorite is Psalm 107:20. *"He sent His word and healed them, And delivered them from their destructions."* Isaiah said, speaking prophetically about the reality that Jesus released, "*Surely He has borne our griefs And carried our sorrows; Yet we esteemed Him stricken, Smitten by God, and afflicted. But He was wounded for our transgressions, He was bruised for our iniquities; The chastisement for our peace was upon Him, And by His stripes we are healed."* (Isaiah 53:5) Peter echoes this reality and confirmation of Jesus' life, *"Who Himself bore our sins in His own body on the tree, that we, having died to sins, might live for righteousness--by whose stripes you were healed."* (1 Peter 2:24) Notice that Peter gives healing past tense in this verse. We were healed because healing was purchased.

Another apostle gets involved and says, *"Beloved, I pray that you may prosper in all things and be in health, just as your soul prospers."* (3 John 2) David says in Psalms 103:2-3 *"Bless the LORD, O my soul, And forget not all His benefits: Who forgives all your iniquities, Who heals all your diseases."* The apostle Paul says, *"But if the Spirit of Him who raised Jesus from the dead dwells in you, He who raised Christ from the dead will also give life to your mortal bodies through His Spirit who dwells in you."* Psalm 34:19 says, *"Many are the afflictions of the righteous, But the LORD delivers him out of them all."* Jeremiah said, that the Lord will restore health to us. (Jeremiah 30:17) The apostle James said that the prayer of faith heals the sick. (James 5:15)

I could keep going and fill a whole book on the healing scriptures, and many authors have. Many have dedicated their entire lives to reclaiming this blood-bought truth to the body of Christ. I figure it this way, don't you think the body of Christ should be as healthy as it's head? Our head (Christ) is very healthy, and He said as He is, so are we in this world. Graham Cooke said, *"We don't have a right to be sick – we have a right to be healed."*

**"A fact, not a promise"** *by Kenneth Hagin (Health Food Devotions)*

*"By Jesus stripes, you are healed. You don't have to pray. You don't have to have someone else pray. It's not necessary to pray when you know this fact as you ought to know it. Simply thank God for perfect deliverance.*

*The afflictions in your body were laid on Jesus. And He bore them. You do not need to bear them. All you need to do is recognize and accept the fact that Jesus has already borne you sickness and diseases. Therefore, you do not have to bear them. That's a fact, not a theory. It's a Bible fact.*

*I've heard people say, "Well, I know the Lord promised to heal me." No, He didn't. He didn't promise. First Peter 2:24 is a statement of fact. It tells you what happened. A promise tells you about something that's going to happen. A fact tells you about something you've already received or that's already happened. By Jesus' stripes, you are healed!*

*Once you recognize this fact, then just refuse to allow disease into your body. Every believer should thoroughly understand that his healing was consummated in Christ. And if every believer thoroughly understood that, it would mean an end of chronic trouble in the bodies of believers."* [7]

**We are healed by faith**

We have no problem believing that when we pray with some to receive salvation, they get saved. They are transferred from the kingdom of darkness into the Kingdom of Light. We believe in instant transformation in the spirit and that they are born again. What if we could believe this way for healing? To God it is the exact same thing. It is an encounter of *sozo*. Our healing is received by faith. Salvation comes by grace through faith. (Ephesians 2:8) By now I think I can say that healing and salvation are synonymous. So healing is by grace through faith.

Now we don't get saved in our flesh, we get saved in our spirit or our heart – our flesh will manifest this reality throughout life. In other words, when we pray for salvation and the faith is there, we are saved whether we feel it or not. Remember, we are not feelers, we are believers. Healing is the exact same way. When we pray for healing, we need to believe we are healed, confess with our mouths that we are healed, and receive the gift of healing whether we feel anything or not. Healing is received in the spirit and then manifested in the physical body. I love the concept of the physical body being quickened because of what the Holy Spirit is doing inside of us. (Romans 8:11)

The Lord is patient and intentional. There are times when Jesus is wanting to do more in our lives than just physical healing. He may have a multidimensional approach to what He wants to release. We will know this is the case when instant healing is not the reality. Our response to this should not be frustration; rather, it should be faith, peace, patience, and freshness.

I love that Jesus is my healer. I love that I co-operate with Him as He heals, and I love His perfect work of restoration even if it takes longer than I would originally like. I always believe for instant healing, but if instant healing is not what He is after, I ask Him this question, *"Lord, besides my physical healer, what else is it that you are wanting to be for me and do in me right now?"* Satan doesn't want you whole. It's his job description to kill, steal, and destroy. (John 10:10) Jesus wants us whole. The Hebrew word for wholeness is *shalom*. Shalom is a multidimensional word. It means: sound, complete, whole, healthy, well, safe, tranquil, prosperous, perfect, full, rest, harmony, peace, and settled. This is who Jesus is for us and it's who we are in the provision of shalom.

One recent summer I had pneumonia. I prayed for instant healing as the onset of fever came on me, and my lung started to fill up with fluid. I prayed so earnestly. I remember pacing all around my basement, and I was rebuking, and loosing, and binding…you know what it's like. Then the Lord spoke to my heart and said, *"How's is going?"* It was like He was saying, *"I see that you are being intense and persistent, but how's it working out for you?"* I love strategic prayer, and so I had prayed from every angle imaginable. Jesus simply showed up and basically said, *"What are you doing?"* I felt a little embarrassed, and He knew that; so He said, *"Son, in your life you are going to have lots of battles, and I know that you enjoy the fight, but I want you to learn how to wear the enemy out with your freshness, joy, peace, and patience. Now would be the perfect time to do that. What do you think?"* Of course, I thought that was a good idea, because I am always open to new identities and new ways Jesus wants to reveal Himself for me. So I was sick for a week, and in that week I enjoyed patiently wearing the enemy out with my joy, freshness, and peace. There were times when the pain and discomfort was intense, but I never lost the awareness of the freshness in my spirit. It was wonderful, and I am now carrying this new way of living life with me. Oh, and the Lord did heal me, and encouraged me to release this revelation to many so that they could do the same. I also know that I have an anointing to pray for those sick with pneumonia, because I have had it about seven times in my life. So now I intentionally look for people who have pneumonia so that I can pray for them.

## Physicians are not a second class healing

Paul Mannwarring said, *"Surgery is not a second class healing."* I would concur with that statement. Medical care and medicine is not a second class healing. Jesus taught us to take people that need help to a physician for care in the story of the Good Samaritan. (Luke 10:25-37) Jesus describes what love looks like in this story: seeing someone who needs help, having compassion for them, taking the time to stop and help, bandaging and applying medicine, taking them to a care facility (hospital), and paying the bill for the care. I love that Jesus is very deep in teaching and modeling things of the spiritual, but I also love that He is very practical. We should view physicians and caretakers as vessels being used by God to bring healing. What if we would exercise faith to that end?

My mom had a cancerous lung tumor. She received such excellent care from the doctors and surgeons that she now is cancer free. She received healing. We don't have to dishonor the medical community and advances in medicine to believe in divine healing. What if they are working in tandem? Please don't hear me wrong. I believe in the supernatural power of Jesus to heal right now, and I believe that our first response should be supernatural healing. I also believe that the church should be a healing center. I believe in the Healing Rooms and my best friend received sight in his blind eye from birth at a Healing Room. What if the church and the people of God could extend the walls of the Kingdom by teaming with the medical community? I think that the medical community would be a great place for the supernatural power of Jesus to be released! Thank you Jesus for our medical care facilities!

## **Jesus healed all**

Did Jesus heal everyone in the land while He walked the earth? I would guess that the answer to that question is no. However, Jesus healed everyone who came to Him for healing. Mark 1:32-34 says, *"At evening, when the sun had set, they brought to Him all who were sick and those who were demon-possessed. And the whole city was gathered together at the door. Then He healed many who were sick with various diseases, and cast out many demons; and He did not allow the demons to speak, because they knew Him."* I have heard some say that the many in this passage speaks to the percentage of the sick and demonized that Jesus healed. I believe on the other hand that the many in this passage refers to a number too numerous to count. For example, if I go to a ball game and sit in a crowed stadium, my response to the number of people in the stadium would be many.

Another favorite scripture of mine is, *"God anointed Jesus of Nazareth with the Holy Spirit and with power, who went about doing good and healing all who were oppressed by the devil, for God was with Him."* (Acts 10:38) It is not wise for us to reduce the gospel and the stories of the Bible to accommodate our experience. It seems illogical to think that Jesus healed all because our experience says otherwise. In these moments we adjust our standard to His. Thank goodness the standard is Jesus heals all!

## Five common questions about healing

I want to address five questions about healing in hopes that this might help you, if you have a battle taking place in you right now.

The first question would be, *"Does God cause sickness?"* A simple answer would be that He doesn't have any sickness to give out. He's not sick. Sickness is contagious – it comes from someone who is sick and that wouldn't be God. Secondly, *"Does God choose not to heal?"* When Jesus went to the cross He purchased our forgiveness and our healing. Either His payment was good enough or it wasn't. According to scripture, healing is finished. The third question would be, *"Does God allow sickness?"* I believe a better question would be, *"Do you allow sickness?"* I'll let you answer that question yourself. Fourthly, *"What was Paul's thorn in the flesh?"* I don't know what Paul's thorn was. Maybe it was Jews wanting to kill him, his own memories of being involved with the killing of Christians, loneliness, wanting to have a family, public speaking, I don't know what it was. I know that Jesus didn't have a thorn in the flesh. He didn't model it or teach it; therefore, it isn't the standard that Christ set. We don't go looking for the reason we're sick when Jesus provided for our healing. Lastly, *"What about Job?"* In the story of Job, Satan brought sickness to Job, and God brought restoration. Job had some fear in his life – that very fear was realized. Fear is a powerful thing. Job makes a comment that we celebrate and put music to. The Lord gives and takes away. Then the Lord rebuked Job for his belief system that allowed for the give and take away gospel. What the Lord gives us, He doesn't take away.

**Standing on promise till the end**

I would have loved to be in church the Sunday that Jesus stood up and opened the scriptures to Isaiah 61 and read the prophecy spoken about His ministry. Luke records that Jesus said, *"The Spirit of the LORD is upon Me, Because He has anointed Me To preach the gospel to the poor; He has sent Me to heal the brokenhearted, To proclaim liberty to the captives And recovery of sight to the blind, To set at liberty those who are oppressed; To proclaim the acceptable year of the LORD. Then He closed the book, and gave it back to the attendant and sat down. And the eyes of all who were in the synagogue were fixed on Him. And He began to say to them, "Today this Scripture is fulfilled in your hearing."* (Luke 4:18-21) In hindsight we know that this prophecy, foretelling the anointing of Jesus, was fulfilled. We have four gospels full of the miracles foretold of Jesus in this prophecy. But I want to share a story where a very godly individual stood on the promise of Jesus to bring liberty to captives, and the promise wasn't fulfilled as he thought it would be. The godly individual I am referring to is John the Baptist.

John was a very righteous man who was wrongfully imprisoned. What a beautiful position he was in to claim the promise of Jesus to liberate captives. We know after Jesus' ascension many Apostles were liberated from prison. In fact the authorities had a hard time keeping Peter locked up. The power of God does liberate captives from wrongful imprisonment! I imagine John was sitting in prison wondering why Jesus wasn't who He said He was going to be for him. We see in Luke 7:19-23 that John had to know if Jesus was who

He said He was. *"And John, calling two of his disciples to him, sent them to Jesus, saying, "Are You the Coming One, or do we look for another?" When the men had come to Him, they said, "John the Baptist has sent us to You, saying, 'Are You the Coming One, or do we look for another?' " And that very hour He cured many of infirmities, afflictions, and evil spirits; and to many blind He gave sight. Jesus answered and said to them, "Go and tell John the things you have seen and heard: that the blind see, the lame walk, the lepers are cleansed, the deaf hear, the dead are raised, the poor have the gospel preached to them. And blessed is he who is not offended because of Me.""*

It's interesting to me that when we get in the midst of trial that we get short-term memory loss. John knew Jesus was who He said He was. He experienced the power of the ministry of Jesus in the past, but in the midst of adversity he wanted to know why he didn't get his miracle. Jesus knew that John was about to die and He made a remarkable statement, *"Blessed is he who is not offended because of Me."* In other words, John you're going to die in prison – you need to be focused on who Jesus is, not what He is not doing. We are not to create theologies around what is not happening. We are instructed to stand on the promise until the end. No matter what happens, our response is faith and trust. There is no benefit to giving up and relegating our faith to the current reality of our circumstances. Even if we perish, yet will we believe! Our response to His ability (which is what responsibility is) is to believe until the end. We don't even have a grid for things not working the way our promise says they will. Graham Cooke says, *"It is better to die thinking we can win than to live knowing we cannot."* Blessed is he who is not offended because of Jesus.

**Our identity**

One of the reasons that I am so passionate about the subject of physical healing is that my family has received a prophetic promise from the Lord that our family has an anointing for healing. We are contending for this reality and identity to be resident on our lives. We have already seen miracles take place in this area, but we are not content to stop where we are. We are thankful, but hungry.

One night my son Levi came to me and said that his stomach was in pain. We could tell that he was in a great deal of pain and discomfort. We immediately prayed and pronounced the healing of Jesus over him. Then I went in the other room and started to Google whether or not I could give him Tums, since he is only three. After careful research and conversation with my wife, we decided to give him one Tum. I called Levi over and told him that he should take this medicine to help his stomach feel better. Levi said, *"Jesus already came out of my heart and healed me."* Wow! What a profound theological statement from a child, more than that in fact. Levi had the faith to encounter Jesus as healer. He actually believed that the prayer of faith heals the sick tummy. My response to my son that night was, *"Of course He would, why wouldn't He?"* As a father, I loved watching my son receive the good news of the Kingdom that night in my living room. How much more does our Father God love watching us, with childlike faith, receive the good news of the Kingdom. (Luke 18:17)

Jesus said, *"Go into all the world and preach the gospel to every creature. He who believes and is baptized will be saved; but he who does not believe will be condemned. And these signs will follow those who believe: In My name they will cast out demons; they will speak with new tongues; they will take up serpents; and if they drink anything deadly, it will by no means hurt them; they will lay hands on the sick, and they will recover."* (Mark 16:15-18) We might not do this well quite yet, but this is the standard that we are working from. This is who we are, and we are realizing it.

I have had people ask me why some are not healed after we pray for them. One possible answer may be that they are being healed in process. (Mark 9:17-29) The answer that more accurately answers that question is this – I don't know. One of the most liberating realizations is that we don't need to know. We live in a culture that needs to know everything. Don't try to figure God out; our brain is not capable. We need to be rejoicing in what He is doing whether it's instant or over time. The reality is that we just don't know some things, but what we do know we are responsible for. We do know that Jesus is the healer, and we are healed.

One of the saddest things the American church has done is disqualify people from receiving their healing. The blood of Jesus has qualified everyone to receive healing through faith. Everyone who wishes to receive healing needs to just receive it by faith. The question is how did you get saved? You believed it, confessed it, and received it by faith. You had a need, believed Jesus could meet your need, you confessed the promise, and you received His provision through faith. How you attained salvation is how salvation is sustained!

## Personal Healing Declaration

Healing belongs to me. It belongs to me because sickness is of the enemy. It belongs to me because sickness is a curse, and Jesus redeemed me from the curse of the law. (Galatians 3:13) [Specify sickness] can't stay in my body. By Jesus' stripes, I am healed and whole! (1 Peter 2:24)

We need to regularly be speaking the word of God over our health – because we know we are healed. "*These things I have spoken to you, that in Me you may have peace. In the world you will have tribulation; but be of good cheer, I have overcome the world.*" (John 16:33) We need to come into agreement with the things that He has agreed to. I've decided to let Him decide. I want to declare what He said is finished. Psalm 68:11 – "*The Lord gave the word; Great was the company of those who proclaimed it.*" God has given us the word, and we are learning to come into agreement with it and declare it!

One resource that has been a regular place of declaration over physical health is, *"God's Creative Power for Healing"* by Charles Capps – a small book but absolutely priceless truth.

**Health Declaration: by David Crone**

*"We declare that our bodies are the temple of the Holy Spirit and that God is our healer. We declare that the same spirit that raised Jesus from the dead lives in us and gives life to our mortal bodies. We declare that complete health is the nature of the Kingdom of God. We declare that the stripes on Jesus back are for our healing and that physical health is our Father's will. Therefore, we say, "Enough" to illness, disease and injury. We say "Enough" to cancer of every kind, immune deficiency disease, respiratory illnesses, and diabetes. We say "Enough" to pulmonary disease, brain disorders and nervous conditions. We say "Enough" to heart disease, heart attacks and strokes. We declare that we have had "Enough" and we take hold of the work of the cross and receive our physical health, vitality, and strength."* [8]

## Relational Exercises

- Do you want to be well? This is not as dumb of a question as it sounds. Some people don't want to be healed. Do you want to be healed?
- If you do, start declaring divine health over your body.
- Use the declaration above as a starter, but develop some declarations over your body.
- Identify areas of your body that aren't working properly and start speaking healing and proper function over those areas. Do this out loud! Your body has to hear it.

# Chapter 9
# We Are Free

Galatians 5:1 (NIV) says, *"It is for freedom that Christ has set us free. Stand firm, then, and do not let yourselves be burdened again by a yoke of slavery."* Being set free is an event, but freedom is a lifestyle. Paul is saying that Christ set us free; so live free. We weren't set free to live in bondage to sin, we were set free to live out our true identity in Christ. (Galatians 5:13) Freedom is a lifestyle that is comprised of many choices day in and day out. We are free to choose how we want to live. When we were unsaved and without Jesus we lived controlled by sin, but when we come to salvation through Christ we are set free. We are choosing freedom, because God chose to give us freedom. One of my favorite promises is John 8:36 – *"Therefore if the Son makes you free, you shall be free indeed."*

The reality of the gospel of freedom is that we are free to be dependent on Christ. We live in a culture of freedom in America, but this culture uses freedom mostly to be independent. We celebrate various forms of independence, and think that freedom is the ability to live for self. Freedom in the kingdom is very different, however. Kingdom freedom is the ability to choose to live life dependent on Christ, and dependant on others. Kingdom freedom gives one's life for another. Kingdom freedom is about who we are and how we show up in life. No one else is to blame for who we choose to be, or how we choose to act. Freedom is the enabling grace to make God choices. Freedom isn't a theory, it's a reality. There are no proverbial chains on our life. We are not prisoners to sin. We truly are free. We are as free as we want to be. We choose the level of freedom we want to live from.

## **The flesh and the Spirit**

The flesh and the Spirit are at war with each other. The Spirit knows who we are – the flesh does its best work as it submits to the Spirit. Jesus modeled this beautifully. Numerous times through the gospels we read that Jesus says, *"Not my will, but Yours* (God's) *be done."* He said, *"Everything I do I see the Father do," "I was sent to reveal the Father,"* and other statements to this effect. The flesh wants to make decisions for our lives, but it is sometimes a poor decision maker. The Holy Spirit is a flat out perfect decision maker. We are meant to live from our spirit man in connection with the Holy Spirit in this natural world. The natural, worldly system lives from the flesh towards the natural reality. This is not who we are. Our spirit man and our flesh man are at odds with each other a lot of the time. We are Holy Spirit led in our spirits and this is who we are.

We are practicing who we are. Unfortunately, we can't cast out the flesh – there is no deliverance ministry that can accomplish that. We are working out our flesh. I was teaching in our school of ministry class, and one young lady asked a good question. She asked, *"What good is the power of the Holy Spirit if we have to* (personally) *work out our flesh."* My response was that if we have the Holy Spirit of self control that means we have a self to control. The Holy Spirit has made provision for us to work out our flesh. My wife says, *"We need the power of the Holy Spirit to work out our flesh – it is not something we can do on our own."* I have found that every *"yes"* to our Spirit-led identity in Christ will most often have to be followed with a *"no"* to the flesh. I am so thankful for the gift of the Holy Spirit of self control, and I am relieved that I only get to control me and no one else.

## How much freedom?

How much freedom do we want? We have as much freedom in Christ as we want – it is totally available to us. This statement has the potential to unleash several opposing questions. The question I have is why don't we choose freedom? Scripture is quite clear that salvation, healing, and deliverance are the same provision (sozo). So then why are there areas in our lives that don't work, and what is the Lord's response to those areas?

When I was born again on March 10, 1998, I got delivered instantly of many things, thank you Jesus! But there are also some areas of my life that still aren't working. Those areas used to intimidate me, and were a source of grief and condemnation. I always used to ask the Holy Spirit why He didn't just deliver me of all of those areas right away. My heart is to always please the Lord, and it annoys me intensely how far away I am from being like Jesus. Along the way in this journey I have come to the realization that the Lord wants me to *work out my salvation.* (Philippians 2:12) The very next verse says, *"for it is God who works in you both to will and to do for His good pleasure."* I have discovered that God likes His job in my life. He loves being my savior, my healer, and my deliverer.

Have you ever led someone to Christ in partnership with the Holy Spirit? What a rush! There really is nothing more exciting than leading someone into an encounter with the redemptive work of Jesus! Have you ever prayed with someone and seen them miraculously healed? What a rush that is as well! To see someone's physical body restored at the name of Jesus is so powerful and wonderful! And finally, have you ever seen someone that you've prayed with be set free from an oppressive spirit or behavior? Again, powerful and wonderful! Well, the Holy Spirit is that way with the areas of our life that need help. He loves being our helper! He loves being who He is. He is our deliverer. It's His name, and it's what He does. When the Word says, *"Work out your salvation,"* it is not saying that we're on our own; rather, the next verse says that God works in us for His pleasure! He loves the areas of our lives that aren't working, because He knows that they are the areas of relational connection with us. He values relationship with us. In our future, we have appointments with God who works in us for His pleasure.

Another truth that has been a source of power and encouragement for me is that in my weakness Christ is made strong. 2 Corinthians 12:9-10 – *"And He said to me, "My grace is sufficient for you, for My strength is made perfect in weakness." Therefore most gladly I will rather boast in my infirmities, that the power of Christ may rest upon me. Therefore I take pleasure in infirmities, in reproaches, in needs, in persecutions, in distresses, for Christ's sake. For when I am weak, then I am strong."* I am perfectly strong in my weakness. It just feels good to say that! In fact, because God's strength is made perfect in weakness, weakness is an advantage.

Next time you have an area that isn't working, make that area a point of relational connection and pleasure with you and the Holy Spirit. Remember that Jesus doesn't use shame to lead you to repentance – He loves you. He'd rather use kindness and goodness. (Romans 2:4)

So what questions do you have about your freedom? What level of freedom would you like to enjoy? What's the question in your heart? I call those questions the, *"yeah but"* questions. What is your *"yeah but"* question? I want to address a few of them in this book because I want to see the Holy Spirit release freedom of thought over you.

## What about addiction?

Addiction is a powerful word in our culture, but Biblically, addiction is sin. Can a Christian be addicted? Addiction takes choice out of the equation, but Christ gives us the freedom to choose. Addiction is very real for those who are not in Christ. But in Christ, addiction is just a lie that enslaves us to being victims without choice, stuck in a lifestyle with no control. This is not who we are in Jesus. We choose how we want to live. There is a difference between understanding our need for deliverance and admitting addiction. Our culture blurs these lines. Deliverance is a beautiful relational activity. Knowing Jesus and hearing Him speak truth is powerful. Admitting who I'm not carries no power. Remember, we are believers. Thankfully the Lord has been raising up many ministries and training people to carry tools for freedom. He is committed to our discovery of freedom.

## What about deliverance from evil spirits?

Although there are some cases where deliverance is needed, I don't believe that everyone needs deliverance from evil spirits. Now I am not talking about being oppressed. Oppression is real and sometimes unavoidable; however, oppression is not possession. Some people need deliverance from an evil spirit preventing them from knowing who God is for them. Some people are in the grip of the enemy, and we are responsible to release that grip. Jesus said that we have authority to cast out evil spirits, which means there are some evil spirits that we have to cast out.

Not everyone has a demon though. Some people just have bad behavioral choices and habits that they need to learn to walk out their freedom in a relational way with Jesus. You can't cast out the flesh. It has to be worked out. Some people have to be set free so they can make the choices to be free; others have to use their freedom to make the choice to be free.

**What about generational curses?**

I have a real problem with theology that allows for any curses in Jesus. As believers in Jesus we live by faith and promise not by curse. (Galatians 3:11,14) Because Jesus died on the cross, He took our curses, and released blessings to those whom He justified by faith. (Galatians 3:12-14) In other words, forget generational curses – they can't pass through the blood of Jesus.

We are a new creation – the old is gone and the new has come. How can a generational curse be alive if the old has gone? Some people look for reasons to excuse their poor behavioral choices. This is not who we are in Jesus. Some people find it interesting to examine their past to validate their current dysfunction. It's tragic the lengths that some people go to blame their present on someone else when all along we have the cross and blood of Christ resourcing us to enjoy our freedom in Christ.

**Whatever the question is, Jesus is the answer.**

There are many things that we are learning about freedom in Christ. God is revealing our identity in wonderful ways. There is a clash, or a battle if you will, in the spirit over our identity and freedom. We win. We are not just learning how to get free – though that is of vital importance; we are learning to stay free. We are learning how to abide, and remain in our identity as believers. We are becoming who Jesus says we are.

Whatever your question – let me assure you, Jesus has the answer and He is faithful. He is a gentleman, He will answer you. If He won't answer your current question, ask a better one. He sees our heart, and He is committed to revealing His heart to us. Wouldn't it be worth the struggle to see your identity emerge?

**Relational Exercises**

- What are the questions you have about your freedom? List them out and ask the Holy Spirit to speak to them.
- How goes the battle between your flesh and the Spirit?
- What is your capacity to abide in your spirit in fellowship with the Holy Spirit?
- What would it take for you to believe that the Lord loves dealing with your areas of weakness?
- Declare that you are perfectly strong in your weakness! (Because of Christ in you!)

# Chapter 10
# We Are Overcomers

There has never been a conflict that the Lord has not come out on top. He overwhelms and overcomes everything that resists Him. He truly is invincible. Good thing for us we are in Him. Our experience and our mindset is that victory is inevitable because there is no other way for us to live with God. God doesn't even allow or consider defeat a possibility. In all our processes in life, victory is guaranteed because we are in Christ. If we are in Christ and in the midst of a problem at the same time; then we know that our problem is in Christ too. We cannot be in Christ and not overcome – it's who we are. We are overcomers who like Jesus, make no allowance for defeat; it isn't in our vocabulary and it's not how we live our life. We actually live our life from victory towards our battle. Instead of being overwhelmed by what is against us, we can be overwhelmed by who He is in us and for us. 1 John 5:4-5 says, *"For whatever is born of God overcomes the world. And this is the victory that has overcome the world--our faith. Who is he who overcomes the world, but he who believes that Jesus is the Son of God?"* Jesus says, *"These things I have spoken to you, that in Me you may have peace. In the world you will have tribulation; but be of good cheer, I have overcome the world."* (John 16:33)

We are learning to become overcomers because we have things to overcome. God intends for all learning in our lives to be fun, and it should put a smile on our face right from the start. We are learning that all problems already have an outcome of victory from God's point of view. His response to problems in our life is excitement and joy, and He wants us to consider it joy to face them. (James 1:2) How we face the things that need to be overcome is just as important as the overcoming. If we start with the right perspective, we can fight with the right weapons.

## Our true spiritual warfare

There is no doubt that we are in a fight. We have a real and formidable advisory. Scripture instructs us to beware of the schemes and plans of the enemy, but it also mandates that we win. Scripture says fight the good fight, and a good fight is a winning one. One of the biggest schemes of the enemy is to attract our focus and attention. If he can successfully do that, he then wants to show us how big he is compared to us, and compared to us, he is big. However, he is no match for Jesus.

One of the most amazing discoveries that I have ever found is a place called the secret place. It's a place that I frequent, and I am practicing to remain there. Jesus spoke of this place, and urged His disciples to live from this place – He calls it abiding. (John 15) One of my favorite scriptures is Psalms 91. Psalms 91 puts an address on the secret place. It assures us that there is a realm to live from where we actually live above natural restrictions, limitations, and struggles. It is a place in the Spirit where we are actually live with God in victory over the enemy. It is an address of love. Psalm 23 also is about the secret place.

Unfortunately Psalm 23 has been robbed from some, and then given back to them at their funeral. It's like, Psalm 23 can only happen after we die. Nonsense. Psalm 23 is our inheritance. It speaks of trust, care, peace, rest, restoration, righteousness, fearlessness, closeness, comfort, provision, aide, anointing, overflow, goodness, mercy, and promise. We need these things now. These provisions are our inheritance. These things are available always in the secret place.

I have had some of the most powerful encounters in this place. When we are in this place the enemy doesn't like to come calling. Have you ever been lost in the presence of Jesus? When you were lost in His presence, was anything else in your life bigger than He was at that moment? No – surely not. That place of His presence is in the secret place. I wonder how many have yet to find the door into the manifest presence of the Lord? This place of presence is our lifeline, and our place of the formation of our identity in Jesus.

Even if the enemy knew where the secret place was, he isn't foolish enough to come calling because the one who answers the door will be none other than one of the members of the trinity. When you are in the secret place, you are too busy being overcome with all the things the Lord is doing for you rather than with what the enemy wants to bring against you.

The enemy may not be afraid of you and me, but he's terrified of the Lord Jesus. He has nightmares about the Father, and the Holy Spirit makes him crazy. Just when the enemy thinks that he has outwitted the Holy Spirit, the Holy Spirit totally outthinks and out strategizes the enemy's every move. The enemy doesn't have access to the wisdom of the Holy Spirit because he doesn't have the mind of Christ. The enemy doesn't attack in wisdom, he attacks with instinct. He is against us because he hates the plans of God that we have over our life. When he attacks, we can be thankful that the only reason he is attacking right now is because he sees something that God has planned in our near future, and he is instinctively attacking. Our response is to step into that identity and provision of Jesus and fight the good fight. The Lord is so mighty that the harder the enemy tries, the Lord can't take it seriously because He's too busy laughing at the plans of the enemy. (Psalms 37:12-13)

Another thing I've noticed about the secret place is that the Lord doesn't like to be interrupted when He's visiting and loving on us. He doesn't like being interrupted while we're feasting. We are a people in love. Christianity is about being in love. We don't have to fight as much as we have to fall in love. Here's the look we are going for – awe, rest, peace, joy, and on and on. Graham Cooke says, *"We exhaust the enemy by being loved. We depress him with our joy. We weary him with our peace. We demoralize Him with our patience. We discourage him with our kindness. We overcome him by using goodness. We debilitate him by being faithful to the Lord. We trouble him by being gentle. We dismay him through our faith. We weaken him with our mercy. We intimidate him by our intimacy."*

What if being more than a conqueror means that we are falling more in love with Jesus and your love scares the devil away? Do you know how the Lord scares the devil away? He throws a feast and feeds you. When we feel surrounded by the enemy, or we feel the weight of frustration, negativity, fear, and being critical, it's time to sit down at the table of the Lord and fellowship. When you sit down to visit with Jesus, the enemy rarely is stupid enough to attack, because Jesus doesn't like to be interrupted while He's receiving praise and adoration from us. Jesus paid a price for us to be untouchable, unreachable, and invincible. What if our life in Christ tortures the enemy? What if our relationship with the Lord scares the devil?

Here is a promise I love. Exodus 23:27 – *"I will send My fear before you, I will cause confusion among all the people to whom you come, and will make all your enemies turn their backs to you."* We don't empower the enemy against ourselves. The enemy has no authority because of Jesus. (Matthew 28:18, Colossians 1:16-23) The only authority that the enemy can get is the authority that we give him. He loves using our God given authority against us. Jesus died to give us a new mindset, new heart, and a presence that enables us to overcome. The three most powerful beings in the universe (Father, Son, and Holy Spirit) live inside of us. Overcoming is automatic for them. And, because it is for them, it is for us too. Graham Cooke says that, *"The enemy cannot compete against the fullness of Christ in us."*

Scripture says that we overcome evil with good. (Romans 12:21) We are using the goodness of God and the fruit of the Holy Spirit of goodness to overcome the enemy. God is good, and the revelation of that truth is so powerful that it has the ability to destroy every work of evil against us.

Moses asked to see God, and the Lord showed him His heart, and what Moses caught a glimpse of was the glory of His goodness. (Exodus 34:7) God revealed this goodness to others in the Old Testament: David (Psalms 103:8, 45:8), Nehemiah (Nehemiah 9:17), Joel (Joel 2:13), Jonah (Jonah 4:2), and Micah (Micah 7:18). In the New Testament, we can behold His goodness in our everyday experience in the Holy Spirit. (2 Corinthians 3:7-18)

## **We are more than a conqueror**

Romans 8:37 – *"Yet in all these things we are more than conquerors through Him who loved us."* What is more than a conqueror? Have you ever thought about that? The very definition of a conqueror is someone who overcomes and takes possession by force. So what is more than that? I believe it is taking possession without the fight because of the fullness of our identity and inheritance. As more than conquerors we arrive at a battlefield that is uninhabited by the enemy because He is unwilling to keep losing to the beloved. More than a conqueror means that the enemy doesn't show up because he knows that it would be a futile endeavor. This is the gospel of Jesus Christ for His beloved. Wisdom is seeing our life the way He sees it, and thinking about our life the way He thinks about it, so that we can live life the way He has purposed it.

Romans 8:31-32 – *"What then shall we say to these things? If God is for us, who can be against us? He who did not spare His own Son, but delivered Him up for us all, how shall He not with Him also freely give us all things?*

Philippians 4:13 – *"I can do all things through Christ who strengthens me."*

Romans 8:28 – *"And we know that all things work together for good to those who love God, to those who are the called according to His purpose."*

These three familiar verses give testimony of the power of Christ's provision for us. These verses aren't just cute promises that we have on a magnet on the fridge – they are our lifeline, our inheritance, lifestyle, our weapons, and our declaration.

**<u>He is patient and faithful</u>**

One of the greatest and most wonderful attributes of the Holy Spirit is that He is endlessly patient – almost patient to a fault. The Lord never gives up on us, He is faithful. One of the encounters I enjoy with the Lord is Psalm 37:3 – it's right before the promise of God giving us the desires of our heart. I love the promise of the desires of our heart, but let me show you what is said in the verse before that. Psalm 37:3 – *"Trust in the LORD, and do good; Dwell in the land, and feed on His faithfulness."* I love feasting on the Lord's faithfulness! He is so good and faithful to me. I think that really it's the thing that I marvel about the most in the heart of God. He is faithful. It's a feast of encounter every time I meditate on that wonderful promised provision.

One of the truths that I have discovered in my life is that I am going to eventually say yes to what the Holy Spirit is doing in my life. Sometimes it takes me longer than others, mainly because I get stupid from time to time. But when the Holy Spirit presents something to us or gives us a direction in life, there is only one acceptable answer and that is *"yes"*. He doesn't really listen to our *"yeah buts"*. He just ignores all of that and says, *"Yeah, but I'll be with you."* Our *"yeah buts"* get ignored by the Holy Spirit.

**The victim spirit**

I would like to address one of the most deadly traps of the enemy in regard to our identity. This section of the book has the potential to identify one of the leading reasons why we fail to step into our truest identity in Christ. Those of us who don't overcome fall into the trap of victimization. I will refer to this as a victim spirit which is a state of mind or mentality. Now there might be a demonic assignment and influence of demonic oppression in your life, so the victim spirit may be a demonic presence, or it may be a result of poorly developed thought processes that has lead you to develop a mentality of victimization. Either way, I would like to address it, because it's a killer to identity.

It is good news for us if we can recognize the victim spirit, because if we can recognize it, we can get rid of it. If we identify victim thinking and influence in our lives we can celebrate, because that means it is on its way out the door. The victim mentality is seemingly a mountain or a stronghold of thought. Strongholds of thought deter us from the mind of Christ. When we recognize a stronghold, we do as scripture commands us to do – we cast it down. (2 Corinthians 10:4-6) Jesus encourages us in this process by saying that it only takes a mustard seed of faith to say to the mountain – be removed and cast into the sea. (Matthew 21:21-22) If you see this ugly victim spirit – get your mustard seed out as you read this and be ready to step into your identity.

I grew up in the Midwest, in a very rural area. One of the stereotypes we have is being *"redneck."* I don't know if you are familiar with Jeff Foxworthy, but he has some funny humor about rednecks. Sad to say I resemble a lot of his remarks. I want to introduce some behavior patterns and characteristics of the victim spirit similar to how Jeff Foxworthy characterizes potential rednecks. So I will list them out as a, *"You might be affected by the victim spirit if…"*

**You might be a victim if…**

- Life happens to you instead of you happening to life. We are believers whose job it is to happen to this world. No weapon fashioned against us can prosper. (Is. 54:17)
- You might be a victim if you give the enemy your power to use against you.
- You might be a victim if you give your power to others who are influenced by the enemy, and in tandem with the enemy, they use your power against you.
- You might be a victim if the quality of your life is in other people's hands.
- You might be a victim if your focus is on your past not your future.
- You might be a victim if you concern yourself with how things should have been.

- You might be a victim if you are pre-occupied with problems.
- You might be a victim if you are always blaming someone else for the way you are.
- You might be a victim if you think you are helpless.
- You might be a victim if you feel you have to control, or have no say over anything.
- You might be a victim if you feel like you are a pawn in the game of life.
- You might be a victim if you use the expression, *"if only", "what if", "I can't",* or *"God can't unless".*
- You might be a victim if you feel like you are always being picked on.
- You might be a victim if negativity controls your thought life.

Our thought life is so important. Philippians 4:8-9 says *"Finally, brethren, whatever things are true, whatever things are noble, whatever things are just, whatever things are pure, whatever things are lovely, whatever things are of good report, if there is any virtue and if there is anything praiseworthy--meditate on these things. The things which you learned and received and heard and saw in me, these do, and the God of peace will be with you."* Does your thought life line up with truth, nobility, justice, purity, love, good news, virtue, and praise? These things are our privilege in Jesus. These things are the environment of heaven, and they are our right in Jesus.

- You might be a victim if you can't seem to take responsibility for your life.
- You might be a victim if you're focused on the natural earth, not the kingdom of God.
- You might be a victim if you don't have a dream and a vision for your life.

**Here are some LESS obvious signs of the victim mindset:**

- You might be a victim if you believe that if someone doesn't like you, it's your fault.
- You might be a victim if someone says something nasty to you and you think that you have done something to offend them and that you deserve this treatment from them.
- You might be a victim if you believe that if you try harder the abuser will love you and stop hurting you.
- You might be a victim if you believe that love is something that you can earn by being who someone else wants you to be.
- You might be a victim if you expect others to accomplish your dreams.
- You might be a victim if you expect others to be responsible for your feelings.
- You might be a victim if you believe that the only way you can change is if other people say you can.

**The negative benefits to a victim mentality**

- Attention and validation
- Don't have to take risks
- Don't have to take responsibility
- It feels right.

Can we give up the right to use our past as an excuse for what we don't have today? That is what it all boils down to! Can we kiss goodbye to all the things that we've held on to that have made us feel good about not doing anything?

**Trauma**

I want to be clear about something that is very real inside the heart of God. The Lord understands our trauma. Trauma is a very real, devastating thing that we don't just ignore. For those of you who have been through traumatic situations, know that you can't ignore them. The Holy Spirit is a master at comforting the brokenhearted, and He knows exactly what our trauma is and how to heal it. Trauma takes time to comfort, and the tender hearted Holy Spirit of all comfort knows this – that is one of the reasons that He never leaves us. Victims are victims because of trauma. Some trauma may be petty and seemingly insignificant for some, but others may have experienced real, serious trauma. As you read, I pray that even now the Holy Spirit is moving on that area, applying specific healing and wholeness to your heart.

## Coming out with promise

When we read the story of the children of Israel we see the victim spirit at work, and we see great trauma and injustice. We need to learn to see ourselves as He sees us. I want to briefly recap this story, and view the response to the healing promise of God.

All throughout this book I have heavily addressed the importance and reality of promise. When the Lord delivered the children of Israel from the hand of Egypt, there was a promise, *"I will give you a land flowing with milk and honey."* (Exodus 3:8) As they left, they were resourced with enough provision to start an entire nation's economy. As they left, they we delivered again from the pursuit of the army of Egypt and led through the Red Sea on dry ground. As they journeyed, they were shaded with a cloud by day, and they were heated with fire by night. When they were hungry, there was manna and quail. When they thirsted, they drank water from a rock. Their clothes never wore out, and their lives were spared from snakes and death.

God brought them to the place where there was a decision to be made. They set out to explore the promised land and destination. There were two responses to the promised land. There is always going to be two responses in our lives. We are either going to say *"yes"* and believe, or we are going to come up with some reason why we can't do what God has promised. It is interesting to me what happens in our minds when we start reasoning away the promises of God. In the story, some of the people wanted to go back to bondage in Egypt. There is something about the familiar comfort of bondage that so many are attracted to. Others said they saw the fruit of the land, and they recognized it was definitely what the Lord brought them to, but there were giants. When you say *"no"* or *"yeah but"* to the Lord, the giants of the land reduce you to the size of a grasshopper. Instead of looking at the giants and saying, *"I guess we get to beat the giants, because we are the children of promise,"* the children of promise returned to a victim mindset that was familiar.

When we say *"yes"* to promise, the victim mindset has to go. There are always two battles we fight. There is the battle to get free, and the battle to stay free. I love the response of Joshua and Caleb. *"Let's take possession; we are well able to overcome it."* (Numbers 13:30) They too were slaves, enduring years of injustice, oppression, trauma, and victimization. What was it in the heart of these two that allowed them to say, *"yes"*? There was a call from the Lord, and we too have this call into something bigger and wonderful. It is our identity. When we say *"yes"* we are saying that we are ready to become the giants in the land. I love that Caleb wanted to inhabit the fortified mountain where the giant enemy would have been the most difficult to overcome. Caleb knew something that we need to learn as well. If God be for us, then who can be against us? Imagine Caleb (a man before the time of Jesus) who didn't have the Holy Spirit living on the inside of him, didn't have Jesus and the Father taking residence in him, but still said I'm a believer. Astonishing. I bet Caleb, sitting in the grandstands of

Heaven as one of the great cloud of witnesses, looks down at us and says, *"What could I have done as a new covenant believer with the Holy Spirit, Jesus, and the Father living in me?"* I love keeping this reality always in front of me, because we have a divine advantage. We don't just have the Spirit come on us and then lift off us; we have a habitational gospel in Jesus. God never leaves us, and He is always in us! This is something worth saying *"yes"* to!

I love the promise that the Lord gave Caleb. Numbers 14:24 – *"But My servant Caleb, because he has a different spirit in him and has followed Me fully, I will bring into the land where he went, and his descendants shall inherit it."* This promise is who we are. Who we are becoming is not only an inheritance for us, but for successive generations to come. As I type these words I think about my children and the momentum that I want to give them with my life, just like the momentum I received from my parents. Our identity is our legacy. We are saying *"yes"* because we have a multigenerational ripple effect in the Spirit over the lives around us. That alone is worth us saying *"yes"* to.

## Truths about overcoming the victim spirit

I want to share with you a list that I found online in my researching the victim mentality. I would like to give credit to the individual who wrote this brilliant work, but I have lost the source of this information and I have been unsuccessful in subsequent attempts to find it. Nevertheless, thank you to whomever wrote this! It has help me a lot and it's my prayer that it will help those who read this book as well.

1. *No one can keep you in your current situation except you. We must begin today to accept total responsibility to become victors, not victims.*

2. *People may have had something to do with how you got in the situation, but only you can decide whether you stay in the situation.*

3. *The victim mentality ends when we take full responsibility for our attitude and direction in life. Deuteronomy 30:15, 19 says, "See, I have set before you this day, life and prosperity and death and adversity…so choose life, that you and your descendants might live (the victorious, abundant, God-kind of life)."*

4. *Ask the Holy Spirit to help you. Full responsibility doesn't mean we're in it alone. God is on our side and He will help us. It's natural to look for help – but let's get it from God. John 16:13 says the Holy Spirit is "Our Helper"! When you have His help, you don't need to blame anyone for anything! We blame when we're helpless – but we're not!*

5. *Understand the root word of "responsibility" is response. We may not be able to control everything that others do to us, but we can control our response. In our response lies our freedom and growth.*

6. *Don't give away your power. We give away our power to live in victory, health and success – when we allow others to determine how we respond. We have the power to choose; the power to forgive; the power to recover; the power to overcome anything. When we blame others, we give away that power to them.*

7. *Take charge of what God has given you. The master said to the servant who hid his talent: "Why didn't you at least invest my money so I could have received interest?" (Matthew 25:24-27) He blamed the master, and excused himself. As a result, he fell to*

*the temptation of resentment and fear. He lost everything because he had a victim mentality.*

**Think it & Speak it:**

*No one can keep me down!*

*I am not a victim. I am a victor. I take full responsibility for my responses in my life – my attitudes and my decisions.*

*God has set before me prosperity or adversity. He has given me the power to choose. I choose prosperity!*

*Holy Spirit, I am asking for your help. You live in me, and you are my Helper! I refuse to give away my power by blaming others. I choose to respond to live with God's Word.*

*I take responsibility for my thoughts, my actions and my reactions. I abandon the idea that my situation is the fault of anyone else.*

*I am an overcomer. I am more than a conqueror through God's great love.*

**Ready to overcome!**

Every one of us has to ask ourselves the question, *"Do I want to be whole?"* All of us love healing, but mysteriously not all of us want to live in wholeness. This is not who we are. Fortunately, our past can be healed and our future can equip us to be whole. The proper direction for our life is forward and upward. Our identity is discovered as we move forward and upward. We have promises, the Word of the Lord, the goodness of God, the nature of God, the power of the Holy Spirit; in what way are we not going to overcome?

## Relational Exercises

- What is in front of you right now that is waiting for you and Jesus to overcome?
- How are you defining the nature of God towards you?
- Are you ready to overcome?
- Are you ready to be more than a conqueror?
- What is keeping you from saying *"yes"*?

# Chapter 11
# We Are a Royal Priesthood

## Worship is our response

Worship is our response to who God is. Worship gives us the ability to see and perceive God in His glory, and when we see Him as He is, we are transformed into His likeness. 1 John 3:2-3 says, *"We know that when He is revealed, we shall be like Him; for we shall see Him as He is. And everyone who has this hope in Him purifies himself, just as He is pure."* Have you ever been lost in His presence, worshipping and adoring Him and been filled with anxiety at the same time? It's impossible. When we are beholding, celebrating, and rejoicing in who He is, we automatically refocus our perspective onto Him. When we worship and focus on Him, we get changed into His likeness because proper perception of who He is occurs. What if worshipping, adoring, rejoicing, and celebrating in Jesus is the quickest and easiest way to step into our identity? Beholding Him in His presence, and being worshipers is our greatest privilege in life. It is hard to fathom that the God of everything actually allows me to worship and behold His glory. The God who doesn't need anything desires that I come and worship Him – mindboggling really. How is it that we've been qualified to actually behold this God of glory and greatness? It is because of Jesus' work of restoring our relationship and identity as ministers to God.

Worship is a matter of identity. John 4:23-24 says, *"The hour is coming, and now is, when the true worshipers will worship the Father in spirit and truth; for the Father is seeking such to worship Him. God is Spirit, and those who worship Him must worship in spirit and truth."* The father is seeking worshipers not just worship. We are worshipers, and worship is an expression of who we are. We have a ministry not just to the world, but we have a ministry to God. We are a royal priesthood. 1 Peter 2:9-10 says, *"You are a chosen generation, a royal priesthood, a holy nation, His own special people, that you may proclaim the praises of Him who called you out of darkness into His marvelous light; who once were not a people but are now the people of God, who had not obtained mercy but now have obtained mercy."* Priests have two responsibilities: they minister to people and to God. We don't just sing songs about God, we actually sing songs directly to God. We are primarily worshipers caught up in worship. To not embrace this identity is to relinquish the reason we exist. God created us to be and to exist for the purpose of His perfect design. Being a worshipper is an original built-in design.

**We are kings and priests**

Revelation 1:6 – "*To Him who loved us and washed us from our sins in His own blood, and has made us kings and priests to His God and Father, to Him be glory and dominion forever and ever. Amen."* We are kings and priests of our God. The man in the Bible that personified a king and priest all in one would have to be King David. David modeled well what it means to be a royal priest in the midst of knowing that the kingly priesthood is a costly identity. David lived his life for God at his own expense. If we are going to bring a sacrifice of praise; then there is a cost involved.

2 Samuel 24:18-28 (NKJV) – "*And Gad came that day to David and said to him, "Go up, erect an altar to the LORD on the threshing floor of Araunah the Jebusite." So David, according to the word of Gad, went up as the LORD commanded. Now Araunah looked, and*

*saw the king and his servants coming toward him. So Araunah went out and bowed before the king with his face to the ground. Then Araunah said, "Why has my lord the king come to his servant?" And David said, "To buy the threshing floor from you, to build an altar to the LORD, that the plague may be withdrawn from the people." Now Araunah said to David, "Let my lord the king take and offer up whatever seems good to him. Look, here are oxen for burnt sacrifice, and threshing implements and the yokes of the oxen for wood. All these, O king, Araunah has given to the king."And Araunah said to the king, "May the LORD your God accept you." Then the king said to Araunah, "No, but I will surely buy it from you for a price; nor will I offer burnt offerings to the LORD my God with that which costs me nothing." So David bought the threshing floor and the oxen for fifty shekels of silver. And David built there an altar to the LORD, and offered burnt offerings and peace offerings. So the LORD heeded the prayers for the land, and the plague was withdrawn from Israel."*

One of the valuable attributes in the heart of a royal priest is that we won't offer our worship to God unless it costs us something. Is your worship costing you something? It can be really easy in our churches to walk in and have our worship cost us nothing. David says it best when he said, *"I will not offer anything to God that costs me nothing."* Maybe our cost is our expression, maybe it's our attitude, our preference, time, inconvenience, whatever it is – worship is about sacrifice. I remember when I was little, my family would stand up for worship. I remember sitting down and my dad insisted that we stand. One Sunday I sat down even though I knew we were to stand. We stood to honor the Lord. I sat down and told my dad that I was tired. He knelt down and pointed out this precious, ninety some year old woman in our church. She and her husband were standing. He told me that if she was strong enough to stand, I didn't have an excuse. There is something to be said about our posture in worship. I'm not about legalism, but I will say that I am about honoring the Lord when He's corporately in the room. It has to cost us.

## Leading captivity captive

It was an Old Testament custom of many victorious nations to lead captivity captive. David wrote about this in Psalm 68, and Paul the apostle echoed this in Ephesians 4. I have always wondered what it meant to lead captivity captive. David modeled this when the Ark of the Covenant was brought up to Mount Zion in 2 Samuel 6-7 and 1 Chronicles 13.

When you see the phrase *"leading captivity captive"* in the Bible, it is referring to an event involving the victorious return of a king from battle, where the whole city celebrates with a parade. When the victorious king would arrive, He would bring with him the spoils of war, and the enemy king or soldiers. The victorious army would parade the enemy king and his soldiers in front of the army in a very humiliating way. The conquered king would have been stripped down naked and jeered, often forced to dance and act *"undignified"* as part of his humiliation. David, though he was the victorious king took the form of the conquered king and a slave. David stripped down naked in reverent humility to the conquering King and danced in front of the Ark carried by the priest into the city.

What a prophetic demonstration of worship! David was a true king and priest of God. David danced with all his might for nine miles in front of the Ark in nothing more than a bib, in celebration of the triumphal entry of the Ark of the Covenant, which represented the presence of God. In the culture of that time, David's actions would have been depicted as completely and outrageously inappropriate and humiliating, which is why Michal,

David's wife, was so disgusted with him. Royalty would not act that way. She rejected David's identity as king and priest, and as a result she was barren. It is easy to dismiss our identity as kings and priests because we don't believe such demonstrative actions are a part of our personality or accepted cultural behavior, but we need to understand that God takes this part of our identity seriously. Our identity as kings and priest is one avenue where the Lord literally births things in our lives. Michal's disgust with David's demonstrative worship resulted in barrenness and rejection. It is not wise to frown with disgust on what God says is the key to our identity and breakthrough.

David's identity of king and priest not only demonstrated bizarre acts of worship, but caused him to do something illegal. When David restored the Ark of the Covenant to the country, he created an open tent where there was twenty four hour ministry to the Lord, as opposed to what the Law of Moses called for. Keep in mind that the Law of Moses was given to Moses by God. Yet David's revelation into the identity as a king and a priest of the Lord called for regular worship of God and that the presence of God's glory would be visible to everyone who would stop to see it. David knew the power of seeing the glory of God. Then God promises in the last days to restore David's tent, not Moses tabernacle. (Amos 9:11) God is inviting us to behold the glory. He knows that our identity as kings and priests release the glory of God in our lives. We are kings and priests. In other words, we are a royal priesthood!

## Demonstrative worship

The closest story in the gospels we have about a church service that Jesus attended is recorded in John 12:1-8. There was a gathering of all types of people in that service: Pharisees, disciples, and the friends of Jesus including Mary, Martha, and Lazarus. People came to this service to hear Lazarus speak about being raised from the dead. However, when Jesus came on the scene the service changed drastically. Mary broke into demonstrative worship and poured the valuable fragrance of spikenard on Jesus. It was worth about one year's wages. When she did that, her wild worship exposed hearts in the meeting.

Have you ever noticed that someone who has bizarre demonstrative worship, worship that is outside the box, will actually expose the heart attitude of everyone in the meeting? Mary released a worship anointing that changed the entire atmosphere in the meeting. Mary did not come to hear a sermon from Jesus. Jesus was the best speaker and teacher in history, but that was not why Mary was in the meeting. When Jesus is in the room we shouldn't be quick to get to the sermon. There is no substitute for an entire congregation's act of worship and adoration. Mary was there to minister to Jesus. Many come to get ministry from Jesus. Jesus loves to minister to us, but Mary knew who she was as a royal priest of the Lord. What if sermons weren't meant to expose hearts? What if the worship anointing and the fragrance of reckless worship was meant to exposes hearts? When Jesus is in the room receiving our adoration, not only are our hearts exposed, His heart gets exposed too. What if the only way to know Jesus' heart is to expose His heart through ministering our worship and releasing our adoration of Him? What if the only way to meld our hearts together is through thanksgiving and celebration? What if the quickest and easiest way to get breakthrough for change in your life is through rejoicing and praise?

Our praise, celebration, adoration, worship, thanksgiving, and rejoicing in Jesus is our privilege. It's our lifeline; it's our breakthrough; it's our access to God's heart; it's who we are, and it's our greatest asset in the kingdom. The center of the church is the throne of God. When we make that a reality, we'll hear twice as much coming out of the pulpit. When the pulpit is the center of the church we'll end up getting wrapped up in cerebral intellectualism and cranial theology. Then we'll develop our own personal theology based on preference, and we'll divide because we value our agreement around thought rather than our unity in spirit.

Mary came to minister to Jesus. Have you noticed that every time Jesus shows up in a meeting we want to put Him to work? Mary didn't come to make a request of Jesus. Miracles, signs, and wonders in the presence are so awesome, but the Lord is seeking worshipers. We need to be worshipers committed to worshipping and here's the thing: worshipers have no problems with signs, wonders, and miracles. They walk in them as an everyday experience. The aroma of their lives is what releases the authority, anointing, and the authenticity of Jesus. When the Lord shows up in a meeting, He loves receiving our praise, and He can't help but give to His beloved! It's who He is. Heaven moves when we accurately respond to who He says we are. In other words, when we live out of who He says we are, His response to us will be a demonstration of who He is for us!

Mary did not come to fellowship with believers; she came to fellowship with the Believed. This doesn't mean that fellowship is bad. We really need one another. There is something powerful about the reality of being in fellowship together corporately with God. God designed corporate worship times to be powerful. There are things we just can't get outside of corporate worship times.

Mary did not come to be refreshed; the oil was for His feet. She anticipated that the road ahead of Jesus was going to be grueling, and so she refreshed Him. This worship was done in the midst of the religious and the political people who were about to turn on Jesus. Mary was not concerned with the religious folk; she was focused on her King and released her demonstration of worship without hesitation. God loves it when His worshipers decide that they are not going to be swayed by religion or popular opinion, but they are going to release their demonstrative worship. Whether she knew it or not, she was sharing in His rejection with her worship. When we know who we are as royal priests, we are able to release His presence, release revelation, release the miraculous, maintain the unity of the Spirit, share in His rejection, and minister to God.

## Worship is about passion

Passion is intimidating to a religious spirit. People lack passion because passion is sacrificial to people who aren't in love. However, when someone is in love, passion is the easiest thing in the world. An act of passion may be deemed ridiculous to a bystander, but passion always makes sense to people who are passionate. Passion moves whatever is in the way to make room for itself. Passion thinks outside of logic and reason. Passion is only understood by people with like passion because passion speaks its own language.

## Being worshipers is intentional

One of the reasons we should be intentional about worshipping, and we should take so much time during our services to worship is we are giving God our priority. We are intentional about the responsibility to be worshipers ministering to God. There are some who haven't received the revelation that we are worshipers. If you lack that vision for your identity, worship to you is something different. In fact, church to you may be something different. You may have this revelation about worship. Ephesians 5:19-20 – "*speaking to one another in psalms and hymns and spiritual songs, singing and making melody in your heart to the Lord, giving thanks always for all things to God the Father in the name of our Lord Jesus Christ, submitting to one another in the fear of God."* Colossians 3:16 – "*Let the word of Christ dwell in you richly in all wisdom, teaching and admonishing one another in psalms and hymns and spiritual songs, singing with grace in your hearts to the Lord."* Your revelation of worship may be a hymn-sing where you get mutually encouraged in the Lord. We spend a little time singing about God, and then we feel the goostickle and we move on to the spiritual stuff – the preaching. Let's get to the word may be your priority. If this is your revelation, I would like to suggest to you that your identity is lacking the revelation of your call into the royal priesthood.

Now the hymn-sing is Biblical, and there is a place for that. We not only use music to teach and encourage people, but we are to take music and offer it up as a sacrifice to God. But, when we lack the revelation of our identity as worshipers, we go to church to encourage each other in the Lord relationally, and forget the primary reason for our gathering – to minister to the Lord.

## Stewards of Joy

The environment of Heaven is filled with joy. The Kingdom of God is righteousness, peace, and joy in the Holy Spirit. (Romans 14:17) Joy is accessible to us as believers all the time. We have the privilege of living lives of joy, and it is what sets us apart from the world. People should know if we are a believer based on the level of joy we walk in. We all want power, but we all need strength. The joy of the Lord is our strength. (Nehemiah 8:10)

Our circumstances in life do not dictate what level of joy we walk in. So how much joy do you manifest in your

life? You have control of how much joy you have. The correct response to the problems in life is rejoicing. Habakkuk says that rejoicing releases joy. Habakkuk 3:17-19 says, *" Though the fig tree may not blossom, Nor fruit be on the vines; Though the labor of the olive may fail, And the fields yield no food; Though the flock may be cut off from the fold, And there be no herd in the stalls-- Yet I will rejoice in the LORD, I will joy in the God of my salvation.*
*The LORD God is my strength; He will make my feet like deer's feet, And He will make me walk on my high hills."*

Rejoicing is the highway that joy comes through. Rejoicing is a choice; joy is the outcome. What does it mean to rejoice? The word means to exalt [9]. When we focus on how wonderful the Lord is, and get into position with His goodness, we are rejoicing. Bill Johnson said, *"If you're waiting on your feelings to get joy, you'll only have joy in seasons. If you believe for joy, you'll have it all the time."*

Of all the promises we have as Christians, our access to joy may be the greatest promise. When everything is working against us, joy propels us to another level. Joy should never be lost in our circumstances. There is a provision in the heart of God where joy never runs out. Isaiah 61:7 says that <u>everlasting</u> joy is ours. Joy is built into who we are in Christ. (Galatians 5:22) We need to understand that God is not passive about joy in the life of believers, because it is one of the biggest provisions He has made for us in Jesus.

1 Peter 1:8 says, *"Though now you do not see Him, yet believing, you rejoice with joy inexpressible and full of glory."* Joy can be obnoxious to people who don't have it. I use to hate when people would laugh in the spirit. I thought it was so rude. Now I think it's contagiously wonderful. I remember leaving a church once because

there were people laughing in the spirit. I think back on it now and think that it was weird that I got offended at people being happy.

Laughing in the Spirit is actually quite Biblical. In fact, the Bible refers to the word mirth. Mirth is mentioned one hundred thirty three places in the Old Testament as a noun and twenty seven places as a verb. The definition of the word mirth is glee, hilarity, merriment, jollity, joviality referring to the gaiety characterizing people who are enjoying the companionship of others. Mirth suggests spontaneous amusement or gaiety, manifested in uncontrolled outbursts of laughter. It's an effervescence of high spirits or exultation, often manifested in playful or ecstatic gestures; it may apply also to a malicious rejoicing over mishaps. Mirth is glee over the failure of a rival. It is hilarity implied by noisy and boisterous joy, often exceeding the limits of reason or propriety. It is merriment of fun, good spirits, and good nature. It's a sound resounding with music and sounds of merriment. It is the atmosphere of festivity, ease, and boisterous hilarity. It is generated by people who are hearty, generous, benevolent, high-spirited, warm hearted friends. [10] This exactly defines the experience of our joy.

What if one of the biggest weapons in our hand was laughter? What if our laughter is our greatest agreement with God in warfare? Ps. 37:13 says that the Lord laughs at the enemy! What if joy is the catalyst that takes us from our problem to the promise of all things working together for good to those who love God and are called according to His purposes? What if joy could take us into a place with God where faith could rise rather than unbelief, doubt, anxiety, and fear? What if joy was the cure for unbelief, doubt, anxiety, and fear?

What if there was 90% more joy in your life than you are experiencing right now? What is the level of your joy right now? What are the things in your life right now that could use a heavy dose of laughter? What if joy is one of the needs you get met in Christ Jesus? What if joy releases you into faith – into a higher level of relationship to God? What are the provisions that can be accessed through joy? When is the last time you came to church and sat during worship and just took pleasure in the happiness, joy, and pleasure of God? When is the last time you let your heart go in worship, in praise, in adoration? What if joy is in you right now and you just need to let it out? What if joy is the avenue to a greater understanding and experience of the love of God? What if you're supposed to be one of the happiest people on earth? What is standing between you and rejoicing as a lifestyle? What would it take for you to travel with more joy? What would it take for you to view everything with a positive outlook? What would it take for you to learn to live in the delight that God has for you? What would you say to being traumatized by joy?

The priesthood of the Lord is marked by the reality of joy!

## Practicing our identity

One of the greatest hurdles to get over in establishing our identity is this: If my identity in God is who I am, and it's supposed to be natural; then why doesn't it feel natural? Here's my explanation for this. We are practicing. With much practice things start to feel natural. Six years ago I started working in the flooring business. If it goes on the floor, we install it. When I first started, I didn't know what the heck I was doing. It was very unnatural to me. It felt like I worked four times harder, and only got half as much accomplished. It was a humbling and awkward experience for quite a while.

Now I am a floor-laying professional. I feel very natural installing any kind of flooring there is, and could lay nearly any product without much thought. I practiced my identity as a flooring installer, and now I'm the flooring guy. In the same way, we practice our identity. If it doesn't feel natural at first, it will eventually. Give it several months, and what you had to work four times as hard at will come to you with little to no effort!

This may come as a shock to you, but feelings are not an accurate gauge of what is natural in the spirit. Feelings are anchored in this natural world. Our affections belong to Jesus, no matter how natural it feels at first. Satan loves to lie to us in our feeling department. We are believers – the feelings will align with our correct belief systems. We may not feel like living a life of celebration. Rejoicing may be a foreign feeling. Thanksgiving with praise may feel next to impossible, but it is who we are. Philippians 4:4 says, *"Rejoice in the Lord always. Again I will say, rejoice!"* 1 Thessalonians 5:16 says, *"Rejoice always, pray without ceasing, in everything give thanks; for this is the will of God in Christ Jesus for you."* What does it mean to rejoice? Rejoicing is intentionally responding to His joy!

In the natural world, rejoicing happens when something wonderful happens. It seems natural for us to celebrate and rejoice when things are going our way. In the Kingdom we rejoice because it is how we tap into the joy of the Lord. Our rejoicing releases the presence of God over our lives, circumstances, and problems. It is the joy of the Lord that is the strength we need to endure. We need to learn to rejoice, because it is our ministry to the Lord, it is our response of faith in His ability, and it is our breakthrough into limitless strength. Practicing how to rejoice when we don't feel like it is crucial, because we are worshipers ministering to the Lord in faith.

## Relational Exercises

- What is your current revelation of worship?
- When is the last time you upgraded your experience of worship?
- Define the biggest problem in your life right now. Begin rejoicing until you are full of the joy of the Lord. Declare that the joy of the Lord is strong enough to carry you through this problem. Repeat every day until breakthrough comes.
- Practice smiling and laughing until it hurts.
- What would demonstrative worship look like in your life?
- What gets exposed in your heart in the face of demonstrative worship?
- Do you value the pulpit more than the Throne of God?

# Chapter 12
# We Are In the Family Business

This chapter includes a number of identities. The best way to describe them in a nutshell would be to say that we are in the family business. God relates to us as His family, and He loves doing His work through His family. I have briefly mentioned earlier in this book about the roles of each member of the trinity. I love how they work together. I love the honor that the Father gives Jesus. I love that He loves blessing and resourcing Jesus. I also love how Jesus modeled the heart of Father, daddy God. I love that scripture says that Jesus was the exact representation of the Father. (Hebrews 1:3-4) I love that Jesus sacrifices His agenda and submits to the Father in love. I love how Jesus persevered to ensure our right to be called a son or a daughter of God. I love the importance that Jesus puts on the Holy Spirit, and I love how the Holy Spirit has dedicated His entire existence to revealing Jesus. I love heaven's family. I am absolutely awestruck everyday that I am actually adopted into this family – that the Father is actually my Father God!

## God the Father

A friend from our church was visiting with me recently and shared with me that he struggles to call God, daddy. This man has a rich history with the Lord, and is a strong man of faith. But like him, many of us have been raised to have a single dimensional view of the Father. We tend to find it easier to reverence this great and powerful God of ours, and rightfully so. He is God, and we are to reverence the Lord God. But Jesus also revealed a heavenly Father that we even approach in love as one would approach his earthly dad. Even so, it seems hard at times for us to relationally co-exist with the awesome God we are to reverence and the Father we come to know as our daddy. God has many dimensions. He is the sovereign Lord of all, and He is also our friend. Thankfully, we don't have to down play one side of God to honor the other; we honor Him for exactly who He is. I am sure that we all have seen folks that have wrongly related to God. We are learning how to exist in His glory while reverencing that glory, and we are also learning to exist in His wonderful love and affection! We are His kids, which makes Him our Daddy! He actually wants us to approach Him with child-like affection.

One of the hallmarks of Jesus is that children loved coming to Him. Jesus (perfectly representing the heavenly Father) said that we actually receive the Kingdom as a child. There is something important and powerful about a little child. We are His children and He sits with open arms waiting for us to crawl onto His lap and receive blessing from Him.

## Inheritance

Children have an inheritance. In the natural, inheritance is released when a death occurs. Jesus died, and so did we when we became born again – we died to sin, and we rose in newness of life. At that precise moment our inheritance was released to us.

Romans 8:14-17 – *"For as many as are led by the Spirit of God, these are sons of God. For you did not receive the spirit of bondage again to fear, but you received the Spirit of adoption by whom we cry out, "Abba, Father." The Spirit Himself bears witness with our spirit that we are children of God, and if children, then heirs—heirs of God and joint heirs with Christ, if indeed we suffer with Him, that we may also be glorified together."*

This passage is loaded with truth regarding our identity. I love my position as son, heir, co-heir, and partaker of His nature. We are heirs of God, which means we have an inheritance. Identity is about stepping into that inheritance. I love inheriting things from the Lord. Our inheritance means that we are resourced by God with blessing that we don't have to work for. An inheritance is not something we earn; it's something that someone else earned. The Lord wanted us to get this valuable piece of identity because He said that we are not only heir but joint heirs with Christ. The question is what was Christ's inheritance? I will let you unpack that for yourself. A verse that appears regularly in this book says that as Christ is, so are we in this world. (1 John 4:17)

## Family matters

I love being a dad, and I'm crazy about my kids. My kids have some things going for them that maybe they don't even know about, but they enjoy all of the time. They get their needs met. Their inheritance from me from the moment of conception was that they were getting their needs met. I have loved watching the process of their development as it relates to getting their needs met. When they were first born, they cried or whined as a response to a need. As they grew older they begin to understand and experience the consistency of their needs getting met and they learned to ask. Then as they grew older they began to go to take initiative to meet their own need.

They automatically know that the provision we have in the house is theirs – they have access to it, and the answer to their need is always *"yes"*. When they mature into teenagers they will start to make food by combining ingredients from the resource centers known as the fridge and pantry. This is exactly how Kingdom maturity happens in the Spirit. The Lord has provision and we access that provision through promise and co-laboring. We don't have to question whether provision is His will. We know it is, and we have access to that all the time.

When my kids leave our house we will never stop meeting their needs, and they have a juicy inheritance coming as well. My wife and I have a goal set so that our kids (when they leave home) have a trust fund set up to provide for things like college, down payments on homes, and maybe it'll fund a ministry habit. We'll never stop resourcing our kids, and we'll never stop loving our kids. When we die, their inheritance will be in full. My children don't have to do anything for us to provide for them except exist in my family. This is the foundation of who we are in the Father's family. We are loved and provided for, but there is a point in time where we grow into who we are and find what we're called to.

It is time that we start counting on the inheritance coming to us in our everyday life. Part of our response to that is that we co-labor to bring in that provision. This is why stewardship is so fun for us! We grow and mature into a place of more because we steward well the place we've been given. There is one thing that I know about the Father; He won't be satisfied until we are living in the inheritance that He has set aside for us. The Father loves confident sons and daughters who know who they are in Jesus, and they move into greater measures of co-laboring roles with the Holy Spirit.

## Owning our inheritance

We need to learn to take responsibility for our own blessing from the Lord. We need to learn to hear from the Lord ourselves instead of constantly going others to hear from the Lord. I have no problem with ministers and ministries that help other people hear from the Lord! I am one of those ministers, and I love being a part of one of those ministries. The goal is to never replace anyone's relationship with the Lord. I never want people to value their relationship with me more than their relationship with the Lord. I am all for helping people, but if you need to hear from the Lord, He's waiting to speak to you personally. Bill Johnson says, *"If you need someone else more than God, you are in more trouble than you think."* God is faithful and intentional to speak to His beloved. He hasn't lost His voice, and He's a gentleman. When we talk, He listens, and when it's His turn to talk, He will. He always responds to our response. God isn't going to give us the silent treatment. We don't have a long distance relationship with God.

If a ministry teaches folks to rely on the ministry more than their personal relationship with Him by listening to His voice, then it's time to rethink that ministry. A ministry needs to be used by God to point people to their own breakthrough, and train them to connect with the voice of the Holy Spirit. Training people to get it themselves is crucial. Successful ministry is about folks learning to be in a healthy vibrant relational connection that allows their identity and inheritance to come to them.

## The poverty spirit

My wife and I have had the privilege of teaching against the poverty spirit in years past. When I refer to the poverty spirit, I am not talking about a demonic spirit, although it may include that. I am referring to a thought pattern or a mentality. A poverty spirit is developed by years of training in mediocrity and lack. A poverty spirit is an enemy and actually wars against who we are in Christ. To be in Christ means it is unacceptable to live in lack. One of the biggest functions of religion is to create a sense of apathy, passivity, laziness, lack of desire and interest.

A poverty spirit works to get as much as it can right now so that it doesn't need to rely on faith. This is a big deal in our walk with God, because so many of us want God to fix everything right now so that we don't have to walk in faith for our needs, and so we don't have to co-labor for our needs. My kids don't eat each meal as though it's their last. They expect to eat three, four, or five times a day. They know that my provision for them won't run out. Likewise, we need to come to an understanding that our Heavenly Father doesn't run out of provision for us.

A poverty spirit says if I have a certain something then everything will be ok. If I have a huge bank account, then I'll be ok. No you won't. I'll co-labor with Christ if I have the resources. No you won't. Here's a big one: I'll give or I'll tithe if I make more money. No you won't. A poverty spirit lies to us by telling us that if we just have more we can be content. When we believe that spirit, we no longer contend for more and greater things, which is the Kingdom.

A poverty spirit is not just about financial things. A poverty spirit lives with small possibilities and small potentials. A poverty spirit restrains God. A poverty spirit is about living at a level of negativity and unbelief towards the promises of God – its living small in the love of God. A poverty spirit will limit our co-laboring with Christ. We are not poor, we are rich. We recognize our need for God, which is what Jesus referred to as poor in spirit (Matthew 5:3), but He meets all of our needs according to His riches and glory. There is only one way to describe His riches and glory, and that is over and above.

There was a crippled man at the pool of Bethesda who lay there for thirty eight years waiting to get healed even though he knew it wouldn't happen. What if we are not waiting around for God to do something; instead, what if He is saying that the ball is in our court? It's like we have this box that we call the sweet someday box. We put all kinds of promises in this box and walk away with this mentality that, *"The Lord's not in a hurry. Whatever will be – will be."* That is a poverty spirit. We are partners with God. We are pulling on the promises of God. God makes provision, we believe it, we confess it, take it as our inheritance, receive it, and enter into it.

Apathy happens when we create a belief system around a past lack or delay in promise. When we are disappointed with any delay in promise, we shouldn't create a belief system about what didn't happen when we believed; instead, it's our job to believe, respond, confess, and enter into promise. Matthew 11:12 says *"from the days of John the Baptist until now the kingdom of heaven suffers violence, and the violent take it by force."* The amplified version says, *"And from the days of John the Baptist until the present time, the kingdom of heaven has endured violent assault, and violent men seize it by force [as a precious prize--a share in the heavenly kingdom is sought with most ardent zeal and intense exertion]."* Ardent zeal and intense exertion is our part; heaven coming is His. All my life people have told me, *"You're a little too zealous."* Well, that's my job – to create a highway for heaven to come down. We are growing and learning aren't we? The Kingdom of God is about passion and desire – it's about pleasure and delight. The heart and will of the Lord is the same. We have some work to do, and we can't get it done by being lazy. My friend and ministry partner Dan has a motto of *"Go big or go home."* Colossians 1:9-12 says, *"For this reason we also, since the day we heard it, do not cease to pray for you, and to ask that you may be filled with the knowledge of His will in all wisdom and spiritual understanding; that you may walk worthy of the Lord, fully pleasing Him, being fruitful in every good work and increasing in the knowledge of God; strengthened with all might, according to His glorious power, for all patience and longsuffering with joy; giving thanks to the Father who has qualified us to be partakers of the inheritance of the saints in the light."* This really is the heart of who we are in Jesus – He knows no other way to be than lavish and over the top!

## Fact vs. Truth

I am not one of those delusional people who is out of touch with reality. I would like to think that I am in touch with His reality. There is a difference between fact and truth. A fact is something that exists and can be seen through observation. The truth is a state of actuality. Although the fact of our life may be one thing, it may not be the truth. For example the fact may be that we lack resources, have a physical ailment, or an addiction – but that isn't the truth. We don't ignore facts, but we greet fact with the reality of truth. This is our co-laboring role with Christ. He provides the truth, and we experience it and the result is realized promise from His perspective and reality. This is our provision in Christ; it's who we are, and what we do.

## Faith is active

What is the one thing that all of us as believers are hoping to hear when we get to heaven? *"Well done, good and faithful servant"* – right? Faith is spelled, d-o; actually, faith is spelled d-o-n-e. We are doers of the Word and not hearers only. (James 1.22) When He speaks we do. We are in the business of manifesting His reality in ours. We all know that faith without works is dead, but did you know that our identity is dormant without faith? We are workers through faith because faith empowers work. I love the *"Hall of Faith"* in

Hebrews 11. Every hero is introduced with a particular description, *"By faith."* They are introduced to us as believers, and then they are described as doers. Our faith is active.

There is a subtle lie in the body of Christ that because God is sovereign and can do whatever He wants, I can't do anything to change His mind. Nonsense. God is sovereign and He can do whatever He wants, but He also has given us the responsibility and stewardship of many things, including our lives. The fact of the case is that there is a will of God which cannot be changed, and there is a will of God that can be. I want to briefly define the two Greek words for the *will* of God.

The first word for will in the New Testament is *boulomai.* The definition of *boulomai* is the deliberate, absolute, purposeful, unchanging, resolute will. *Boulomai* is used thirty four times in the New Testament. The boulomai is the unchanging, inflexible sovereign will of God. [11] One example is that there will be a judgment day. No prayer will change that – it is a set event in the future. It will happen. There are events and circumstances that are determined in the *boulomai* will of God.

The other Greek word for will is *thelema*, which is used sixty four time in the New Testament. *Thelema* is the wishes and purposes of God to bless mankind through Christ. It is what God wishes to be done by us. It is His pleasures, desires, and inclinations. [12] Romans 12:2 says, *"Do not be conformed to this world, but be transformed by the renewing of our mind, that you may prove what is that good and acceptable and perfect will of God."* This verse has three different Greek words to describe the will of God – good (*agathos*), acceptable (*euarestos*), and perfect (*teleios*). In other words, the *thelema* will of God is described as good, pleasing, and perfect by Paul. This will refers to the will of God that we shape. We co-labor in the *thelema* of God.

Jesus illustrates the two wills in Luke 22:42 saying, *"Father, if it is Your will* (boulomai), *take this cup away from Me; nevertheless not My will* (thelema), *but Yours, be done."* Jesus says, Father I want your perfect will, which means He has one. Then Paul says that the Lord also has a good and pleasing will that works through us. Jesus said in John 4:34, *"My food is to do the will (thelema) of Him who sent Me, and to finish His work."*

My point is this – we can't relegate our lives, relationships, and our role in the earth to the *boulomai* will of God. Jesus didn't do that, and it is not in our identity to do that either. We are moving the *thelema* will of God in our lives, relationships, and the earth. Smith Wigglesworth made a very controversial statement. He said, *"If God is not moving, I'll move Him."* This statement is not an arrogant statement, but rather a statement of truth. God was moved for humanity, and we know this because He sent Jesus into the world. Because of the finished work of Christ, our identity now is to partner in His redemptive plan on the earth. We actually move the hand of God because He has given us His name, His Spirit, and access to His nature. We have it all. Scripture say that we are thoroughly equipped for every good work. (2 Timothy 3:17) Ephesians 2:10 says, *"For we are His workmanship, created in Christ Jesus for good works, which God prepared beforehand that we should walk in them."* Whether we know it or not, we're in the family business which is living and spreading the full gospel of Jesus Christ!

**Relational Exercises**

- Do you struggle with knowing God as Father?
- Next time you pray, use Daddy in your prayer and see what your heart response is.

- What is keeping your inheritance from coming to you?
- What are the needs in your life? What could you do to co-labor with the Lord in meeting those needs together?
- Does fact rule truth in your life or does truth rule fact?
- Ask the Father to show you His passion and desire for your life, relationships, and the world around you.

# Chapter 13
# We Are Dreamers

## Imagination

Ephesians 3:20 says, *"Now to Him who is able to do exceedingly abundantly above all that we ask or think, according to the power that works in us."* There are progressions in this verse. The first promise here is that God is able to do more than we ask. What is the ceiling of your asking? At what point in your asking God would you get to a point where it would be asking for too much? God says, He wants to go beyond that.

The second promise is that He is able to do way more than we can think. What is the ceiling of your thinking? At what point in your thinking would you get to the point where your thinking would be out of bounds of what God would reasonably do for you? God says He wants to go beyond that.

What is beyond our thinking? I believe God is inviting us to imagination. God designed our minds for imagination and creativity. Imagination is our ability to think of how God could handle some impossibilities in our life. Imagination is a weapon in our hand – it is a wonderful relational exercise with the Holy Spirit. Our imagination empowers us to live in a world of possibilities. Our imagination is our ability to evict negativity and critical thoughts that come from our environment. Our imagination is a beautiful place of relationship and access to the mind of Christ. What if God can be even more wonderful than we can even imagine? What would that be called? It would be called dreaming with God.

World-changers are always connected to the dream that God has for them. Our faith and our identity grow in a culture of imagination, not logic. God doesn't live in the confines of logic, He is accessed from a place of imagination and dreaming!

## God has a dream for you

There is a dream inside the heart of God for all of us – especially in Christ. His dream for us is bigger than our dream for ourselves. We were meant to live from a place of dreaming into a place of dreams fulfilled. The majority of our life in Jesus should be spent realizing dreams coming true.

Ps. 126 says, *"When the LORD brought back the captivity of Zion, We were like those who dream. Then our mouth was filled with laughter, And our tongue with singing. Then they said among the nations, "The LORD has done great things for them." The LORD has done great things for us, And we are glad. Bring back our captivity, O LORD, As the streams in the South. Those who sow in tears Shall reap in joy. He who continually goes forth weeping, Bearing seed for sowing, Shall doubtless come again with rejoicing, Bringing his sheaves with him."* This is the reality of life in Jesus.

When we are in captivity, what are we dreaming about? Captives don't dream about freedom, they dream about survival. Captives want relief – prosperity is too far off and it is unreasonable. Our dreams are limited by problems because we typically dream on the same level as our problem. God is dreaming about our identity and the desires of our heart.

What is God dreaming over you? His dream is that you would prosper! His dream is for your freedom, prosperity, and peace! What if His dream is your life immersed in abundance? What if living from His dream for us is who we are in this life? What if His provision is connected to our dreaming? We have to start seeing God differently. We are not ordinary. We are products of our environment – our environment is in Christ!

In the last days old men will dream again. (Acts 2:17) In our culture something typically happens to old men – they get cynical in their old age. God is saying here that even old men are capable of living with a dream in their heart, put there by the Lord. It's time to dream again. Amazing power would be released if our old men would disciple the world in how to live from a place of dreaming! I want that said of my life. I want to live in a place of dreaming and dreams fulfilled as a way of life, and I want to champion others in their dreams.

## Think ahead

Forward thinking gives power to our destiny. Forward thinking creates a highway for change to come, and then we get to embrace the new. Forward thinking doesn't dishonor the past. New ideas and change has brought all of us into more and greater. The greatness of our past compels us to grab a hold of our history and honor it by pioneering into new places. If our greatest days are behind us, we've lost the momentum of those who've thrust us into what we now have.

## Living from our future

There is an old adage that says, *"Either get busy living or get busy dying."* Our life in the Spirit is connected to our dreaming. If our future isn't bigger than our past, we are dying. If our future isn't as exciting as our past, we are dying. If our dream in front of us isn't as big as our dreams fulfilled behind us, we are dying.

Our future is not only secured, it is exciting! Unfortunately many live from the bondage of their past. Satan wants believers to live from their past because he wants us time locked so that we are moving backwards instead of forward. The only acceptable movement in the Kingdom is forward and upward. We are not stuck in our past. We are the dreamers of dreams. Dreamers are free and excited to walk away from the constraints of their past into something new. The Holy Spirit wants us living from our future.

The enemy wants us to get pre-occupied with trying to fix what's already happened so that our focus stays in the past. What we focus on, we empower. If we are focused on our past we become a victim of our past. If we are focused on our sin, then we empower our own dysfunction. One the other hand, if we are focused on our destiny, we empower who we are now with who we are becoming! The only one that can benefit from us living in and from our past is Satan.

We are putting the past behind us and pressing on towards the high call on our lives in Jesus Christ. Philippians 3:12-14 says, *"Not that I have already attained, or am already perfected; but I press on, that I may lay hold of that for which Christ Jesus has also laid hold of me. Brethren, I do not count myself to have apprehended; but one thing I do, forgetting those things which are behind and reaching forward to those things which are ahead, I press toward the goal for the prize of the upward call of God in Christ Jesus."*

Who we are now is our identity, and who we are becoming is our destiny. Our identity is a key to our destiny. Knowing who we are in Jesus is the key to unlock our destiny and assignment on earth. Likewise, our destiny is the key to our identity. Our future is the key to our present. It always has been. That's what is so powerful about the prophetic ministry. It speaks into who we are in the future so we can trade what we're not in the present for the glorious future God promises us. The secret to overcoming is not rising above our past, it's embracing our future. Likewise, the secret to growth is not reliving the past successes, it's embracing the new thing God wants to do in you. Future growth is about being able to give up the right to use our past as an excuse for what we are not today. We have the authority to bury those past things. Did you know that we have the choice of whether our past has authority over us, or whether our destiny has authority over us? In every dealing we have with God, what He's doing is revealing who He says we are. His objective in our life is to make us apart of His family and to empower us to live like it. That's why the problem right in front of us is never the problem. Problems are exciting – they are loaded with the possibilities of God!

If your perception of your problem is that the problem is the problem, then the problem is that you think the problem is your problem. That's a problem. Many have focused on problems for so long that even their problems have problems. We shouldn't be too quick to inventory who we are not, instead we should be inventorying who we are in Jesus and who He is in us.

The enemy may or may not contend against your future. When and if he does, you have to contend against him for your future. It's time to live in such a way that it makes our destiny more accessible right now. We are never stuck now. Our destiny is a huge part of our hope. My definition of hope is this: present permission from our future to make a present breakthrough. If my destiny doesn't have chains, restrictions, or impossibilities; then I want to live now with no chains, no restrictions, and no impossibilities. Our thinking has to stop being a playground for the enemy, and start being a place of dreams.

## Our inheritance comes from our Father not our past

Wendy Backlund shared an important truth. She said that, *"A baby doesn't determine its future according to its past. A baby determines its future according to his parents."* Papa God has determined our future inheritance in Jesus, and we are defined by who Jesus is for us in this world. As born again believers we can't base what we can or cannot do in our past. We need to look at our Daddy.

## Time to "think again"

At some point in our lives we have to live above everything that has ever plagued us, made us victims, and haunted us. Our history is not our life; however, our history of overcoming hardships helps us connect others to the dream God has for them. Our ministry is releasing the breakthrough that we have been given in our own lives, and our testimony is fueled by our ability to live in the dream that God has for us.

The primary goal of this chapter is to release the permission of God for you to raise your level of expectation and to think differently about your life. In the Spirit, you are where you are because of a series of choices and thought patterns. If you don't like where you are at in the Spirit, it's time to think again. The word for this in the Bible is *repent*. Repentance means to change your thinking. [4] Repentance is one of the greatest privileges we have in the Christ. Why do we have to be talked into repenting when repentance is a privilege in Christ? I think it's because we dread repentance. When repentance is brought up, many have been taught that repentance is hard and sacrificial. What if repentance could be fun? Jesus sacrificed everything so that we could repent! What if repentance was meant to be as easy as just thinking again? God allows us to change our mind about our choices, our way of seeing problems, and the direction of our life.

It is totally ok for us to think like an overcomer. It is ok for us to think about ourselves the way God thinks about us. It is ok to think in line with faith, peace, and hope. Proverbs 23:7 says, *"For as he thinks in his heart, so is he."* Our thinking and our repentance are the keys in choosing freedom. The cross of Christ gives us the power to choose how we want to think. Because of Jesus, we have the right to live in freedom.

We should not let our thought processes be determined by our past. Our thought processes should be anchored in our present and our future. It is one thing to think properly about ourselves and our circumstances, but it's another thing to know how He thinks about us and our circumstances. We live from Him, through Him, and then towards our life and circumstances.

Knowing that He loves us, He's for us, He's with us, and He has a beautiful plan and dream for our life, empowers us to think from joy and peace inside of His love for us. We are accepted in Christ, and He is faithfully and patiently waiting for us to think again.

Of all of the people on the earth, we are the most blessed and accomplished because He has a dream for us and we are beginning to think of ourselves the way He thinks of us!

**Relational Exercises**

- What are the dreams God has for you? What are your dreams? I bet they are very closely related.
- Spend time thanking and rejoicing over God's dream for you.

- What are you imagining about your future?
- What are the desires of your heart? Ask for them, think and meditate on them, then allow yourself to imagine how God could bring that to fruition. Give yourself permission to daydream about that.
- Continue listing out your identity and inheritance in Jesus!

# Conclusion
# Defining your identity

It is my prayer that the identities I have described and the truths I have shared help you define who it is God is calling you to be. I pray that you embark on a journey into new areas of who the Lord wants to be for you. Before we finish, I would like to share one last tool with you. It's been a joy of mine to define who I am in my journey in Christ. I would like to share that with you. Hopefully, you'll get a declaration and an identity definition for yourself. I've hung this statement on my mirror in my bathroom for two reasons. The first is I want to see it, and declare it every day! The second is that I want to remind myself that as I look in the mirror, I am beholding the glory of God, and I am being transformed from glory to glory. God bless each of you on your journey into the heart of God in Jesus Christ's Name! And have the time of your life becoming who you are in Jesus!

**This is the inheritance and authority in our family...**

We will sow our lives into the destiny of other people, calm each storm of opposition, take each test of life and turn them into a testimony, pursue the impossible, transform the darkest places on earth into the light of the world, see an army in the dry bones, and speak to things as though they will be even though they are not.

We can win a battle with a jar and a torch, and we will carry with us an expectation of exceeding abundantly more and above our comprehension.

Who we are will not be decided by our economy, our government, or persuaded by popular opinion.

We live our lives confidently because of the reality of God's revealed purposes and plans. Even against all hope, in hope will we believe. We are counted among the violent of faith who seek with ardent zeal and intense exertion the precious prize of the Kingdom of our God, while seeking the reality of *"on earth as it is in heaven"* or if you like – the kingdoms of this world becoming the Kingdoms of our God.

We will labor from rest, live life full of His presence, and fill our lives with the atmosphere of heaven. We will live dangerously, worship passionately, love unconditionally, laugh often, and live life traumatized by joy. We are hope peddlers, grace givers, risk takers, fire starters, seed throwers, and dreamers.

Our face is set, our steps are ordered, our pace is accelerated, and our resolve is strong. We will not be detoured, lured away, compromised, bought, deluded, or delayed. We will not flinch in the face of sacrifice, hesitate in the presence of the adversary, negotiate at the table of the enemy, ponder at the pool of popularity, or meander in the maze of mediocrity. We won't give up, shut up, or let up from the great work that our hand has found to do for His Kingdom until He stops us. We will surge ahead with a sword in one hand, a hammer in the other, and the song of praise on our lips. And when He comes for us, He will have no problems recognizing us for our banner is clear – we are the beloved of God!

## Source page


1 – Blue Letter Bible. "Dictionary and Word Search for gnōsis (Strong's 1108)". Blue Letter Bible. 1996-2012. 3 Nov 2012. < http:// www.blueletterbible.org/lang/lexicon/Lexicon.cfm? strongs=G1108 >

2 – Blue Letter Bible. "Dictionary and Word Search for epignōsis (Strong's 1922)". Blue Letter Bible. 1996-2012. 3 Nov 2012. < http:// www.blueletterbible.org/lang/lexicon/Lexicon.cfm? strongs=G1922 >

3 – Blue Letter Bible. "Dictionary and Word Search for ginōskō (Strong's 1097)". Blue Letter Bible. 1996-2012. 3 Nov 2012. < http:// www.blueletterbible.org/lang/lexicon/Lexicon.cfm? strongs=G1097 >

4 – Blue Letter Bible. "Dictionary and Word Search for metanoeō (Strong's 3340)". Blue Letter Bible. 1996-2012. 29 Dec 2012. < http:// www.blueletterbible.org/lang/lexicon/Lexicon.cfm? strongs=G3340 >

5 – Blue Letter Bible. "Dictionary and Word Search for hamartia (Strong's 266)". Blue Letter Bible. 1996-2012. 3 Nov 2012. < http:// www.blueletterbible.org/lang/lexicon/lexicon.cfm? strongs=G266

6 – Blue Letter Bible. "Dictionary and Word Search for hamartanō (Strong's 264)". Blue Letter Bible. 1996-2012. 3 Nov 2012. < http://

www.blueletterbible.org/lang/lexicon/Lexicon.cfm?
strongs=G264 >

7 – Hagin, Kenneth. *Health Food Devotions*. Tulsa: Faith Library Publications, 2002, 2007. Medium of Publication. *"A fact, not a promise."* Page 118.

8 – Crone, David. "Health Declaration." *Enough Declarations.* 26 June 2011. Web. http://www.tmvv.org/resource.html

9 – Blue Letter Bible. "Dictionary and Word Search for `alaz (Strong's 5937)". Blue Letter Bible. 1996-2012. 16 Nov 2012. < http://
www.blueletterbible.org/lang/lexicon/lexicon.cfm?
Strongs=H5937&t=KJV >

10 – Modern Language Association (MLA): "mirth." Online Etymology Dictionary.
Douglas Harper, Historian. 01 Dec. 2012.
<Dictionary.com
http://dictionary.reference.com/browse/mirth>.

11 – Blue Letter Bible. "Dictionary and Word Search for boulomai (Strong's 1014)". Blue Letter Bible. 1996-2012. 16 Nov 2012. < http://
www.blueletterbible.org/lang/lexicon/lexicon.cfm?
Strongs=G1014&t=KJV >

12 – Blue Letter Bible. "Dictionary and Word Search for thelēma (Strong's 2307)". Blue Letter Bible. 1996-2012. 16 Nov 2012. < http://
www.blueletterbible.org/lang/lexicon/lexicon.cfm?
Strongs=G2307&t=KJV >

## Other Books from Sword of the Spirit Publishing

### 2008

*All the Voices of the Wind* by Donald James Parker
*The Bulldog Compact* by Donald James Parker
*Reforming the Potter's Clay* by Donald James Parker
*All the Stillness of the Wind* by Donald James Parker
*All the Fury of the Wind* by Donald James Parker
*More Than Dust in the Wind* by Donald James Parker
*Angels of Interstate 29* by Donald James Parker

### 2009

*Love Waits* by Donald James Parker
*Homeless Like Me* by Donald James Parker

### 2010

*Against the Twilight* by Donald James Parker
*Finding My Heavenly Father* by Jeff Reuter
*Never Without Hope* by Michelle Sutton

### 2011

*Silver Wind* by Donald James Parker
*Their Separate Ways* by Michelle Sutton
*Silver Wind Pow-wow* by Donald James Parker
*The 21st Century Delusion* by Daniel Narvaez
*Hush, Little Baby* by Deborah M. Piccurelli

### 2012

*Destiny of Angels* by Eric Myers
*It's Not About Her* by Michelle Sutton
*The Legacy of Deer Run* by Elaine Marie Cooper
*Decision to Love* by Michelle Sutton
*It's Not About Me* by Michelle Sutton
*It's Not About Him* by Michelle Sutton
*Will the Real Christianity Please Stand Up* by Donald Parker
*Amazing Love* by K. Dawn Byrd
*That Summer* by Jo Huddleston

### 2013

*The Fleeing Tiara* by Dennis Doud
*What in God's Name Are We Doing?* By Dan McGowan
*The Accidental Missionary* by Donald Parker & Chip Rossetti